THE COMPANIONSHIP OF BOOKS

AND OTHER PAPERS

BY

FREDERIC ROWLAND MARVIN

Essay Index

Essay Index Reprint Series

BOOKS FOR LIBRARIES PRESS
FREEPORT, NEW YORK

First Published 1905
Reprinted 1969

STANDARD BOOK NUMBER:
8369-1227-6

LIBRARY OF CONGRESS CATALOG CARD NUMBER:
75-90662

PRINTED IN THE UNITED STATES OF AMERICA

The Companionship of Books

To the Memory of

MY FATHER

AND TO

MY MOTHER

PREFATORY NOTE

THE author of *The Companionship of Books and Other Papers* makes this explanation with regard to the book he now presents to the reading public. The sentences and paragraphs and, in some instances, more lengthy articles which compose this work were written at various times, and many of them have been published in magazines and literary periodicals. To those already published have been added a number that here for the first time make their appearance in print. They sustain little or no relation to each other, and, therefore, admit of only a very general arrangement. The last page in the collection was finished two years ago, but the author did not feel that the work was completed, and could not bring himself to deliver the manuscript into the hands of his publisher. The generous reception, however, given to his *Last Words of Distinguished Men and Women*, and his *Flowers of Song from Many Lands* has encouraged him to place this book upon the list of his published works. Its

Prefatory Note

preparation furnished to him many delightful
hours in the library, and he now sends it forth
with the hope that it may bring to others both
pleasure and profit.

F. R. M.

ALBANY, N. Y.,
May, 1905.

CONTENTS

vii

Contents

Contents

Contents

xi

The Companionship of Books

THE COMPANIONSHIP OF BOOKS

I SAY with Channing, "God be thanked for good books." When all other friends forsake us they remain true. We hear much about select society, but the humblest student can show you upon a single shelf in his library better society and far more select than may be found in all the drawing-rooms of both Europe and America. They who are not invited to Miss Flora McFlimsey's german nor to the Grand Duke's ball may have at less expense an evening with Shakespeare or a dinner with Scott and Burns. They may associate upon the most friendly terms with all the poets-laureate, from the first Versificator Regis to the gifted author of *In Memoriam*. Washington Irving could appreciate the companionship of good books when he wrote:

"The scholar only knows how dear these silent yet eloquent companions of pure thoughts and innocent hours become in the season of adversity. When all that is worldly turns to dross around us, these only retain their steady value. When friends grow cold, and the converse of intimates languishes into vapid civility and commonplace, these only continue the unaltered countenance of happier days, and cheer us with that true friendship which never deceived hope nor deserted sorrow."

There was a time when books were so valuable it was dangerous to have them. Men gave fortunes in the old Greek and Roman days for single manuscripts. An enthusiast would work all his life for a damaged copy of some favorite master; and Christians used to go into bondage to possess a Gospel. One of the Ptolemies starved the Athenians into loaning him the original manuscripts of Æschylus, Euripides, and Sophocles. Jerome, who lived in the fifth century, declared that he ruined himself in purchasing the works of Origen. And yet, standing before my library, which is not a large one, I salute all the worthies of antiquity and the gifted of later years. Let a man love books and at once they flock around him, filling his mind and heart with deathless companionships and with the sweetest of consolations. Leigh Hunt, sitting by his fireside, wrote:

"I looked sideways at my Spenser, my Theocritus, and my *Arabian Nights ;* then above them at my Italian Poets; then behind me at my Dryden and Pope, my Romances and my Boccaccio; then on my left side at my Chaucer, who lay on my writing-desk, and thought how natural it was in Charles Lamb to give a kiss to an old folio, as I once saw him do to Chapman's Homer.''

I have sometimes wondered what books I should choose for constant companions were I forced to make a narrow selection. Stanley, the African explorer, contracted his library, under pressure of travel in a wild country and among savage peoples, to the Bible, Shakespeare, *Sartor Resartus*, Norie's *Navigation*, and the *Nautical Almanac* for 1877. One by one these were discarded, and at last Stanley had only the Bible and Shakespeare left. Savages, mistaking the latter work for a treatise on magic, obliged him to cast it into the fire, and then the great traveller's library consisted of but one book—the best of all books— the Word of God. Viscount-General Wolseley always carried the *Book of Common Prayer*, *The Imitation of Christ*, and the *Soldier's Pocket-Book*. Outside of these he liked best the *Meditations* of Marcus Aurelius. Were I obliged to choose twenty works to be forever my only literary companions, I should select (if I know my own heart, and I am not sure that I do): 1. The Bible; 2. *The Analects of Confucius*,

Legge's translation; 3. *The Mahabharata* and *Ramayana*, in Wheeler's *History of India* (the first volume contains the *Mahabharata* and the second the *Ramayana*); 4. *The Edda*, including early Norse romantic genealogical poems; 5. Homer; 6. Herodotus; 7. Plutarch's *Lives;* 8. Sophocles; 9. Euripides; 10. Æschylus; 11. Shakespeare. 12. Bacon's *Novum Organum* and *Essays;* 13. Eckerman's *Conversations with Goethe;* 14. Bunyan's *Pilgrim's Progress;* 15. Thomas à Kempis's *Imitation of Christ;* 16. Dante, both *Divina Commedia* and *Vita Nuova,* Longfellow's translation of the former and Rossetti's (in *Dante and His Circle*) of the latter; 17. *The Arabian Nights,* Burton's translation; 18. Cervantes *Don Quixote;* 19. Emerson's *Essays;* 20. Burns.

Could I select, in addition to the foregoing, ten novels, they should be: *Gil Blas, Vicar of Wakefield, On the Heights, Ivanhoe, Vanity Fair, David Copperfield, Pickwick Papers, Les Misérables, Adam Bede,* and the *Scarlet Letter.*

We owe much to books, and every year greatly increases the debt. They have preserved to us the treasures of the past, and they constantly awaken within our bosoms aspirations that quicken us to all that is noble in life. They are the best consolers of a wounded heart. To them we may go in the hour of sorrow and of misfortune, and find true and unwavering friendship.

"When evening has arrived," wrote Niccolo Machiavelli, "I return home and go into my study. . . . I pass into the antique courts of ancient men, where, welcomed lovingly by them, I feed upon the food which is my own, and for which I was born. For hours together the miseries of life no longer annoy me; I forget every vexation; I do not fear poverty, for I have altogether transferred myself to those with whom I hold converse."

Roger Ascham, contemplating the children of the chase, exclaimed: "I wist, all their sport in the park is but a shadow to the pleasure that I find in Plato. Alas! good folk, they never felt what true pleasure meant." To one who truly loves and understands good books, and is at home in their society, mean pleasures and base delights become irksome. He who has dined with the immortals can no more relish a meal of carabpods.

The versatile author of the *Augustus Letters* records in the New York *Observer* of May 9, 1901, that,

"In delivering an address on a recent literary occasion in England, Joseph Choate, the American Ambassador, told the story of a visit which was made by Oliver Wendell Holmes to his friend and literary brother, James Russell Lowell, at Cambridge, Massachusetts. Lowell was lying on the lounge, his limbs bent and twisted with rheumatic gout, when Dr. Holmes came in and asked after his health. Lowell cheerfully replied: ' I 've forgotten all about my pains, for I am reading *Rob Roy.*' This was better than opium or cocaine to the man whose keenest enjoyment was found in literature. His life had been spent in the pursuit and cultivation of letters, and as his day declined, amidst pain and trial, books had power to charm away bodily ills or to remove him temporarily from their control."

A French writer assures us that Bourdaloue owed his "masculine and solid eloquence" to the constant study of St. Paul, St. Chrysostom, and Cicero. Grotius had always with him a copy of Lucan, and he never opened the book without kissing it upon both covers. Daniel Webster attributed all his greatness to the Bible, which he said was his "daily study and vigilant contemplation." A dark world this would be were all books burned in some great fire, never to be reproduced. It was a melancholy day for us all, though our great-grand-parents were then in the "womb of the earth," when Omar destroyed in the four thousand baths of Alexandria those priceless manuscripts —a quarter of a million of them—which no scholarship will ever be able to replace. The world is wise enough now to remember with indignation the fate of the picture-writings of ancient Mexico. The missionaries who consigned those precious records of an unknown world to the all-devouring flames thought they were conferring a lasting favor upon mankind, but they were, in fact, guilty of a superstition as gross as that they hoped to disperse in smoke and ashes. No right of conquest can ever sanction vandalism. Antiochus burning the library of the Temple at Jerusalem, Persians destroying the sacred books of the Phœnicians and Egyptians, Romans burning the books of Jews and Christians, Jews tearing to shreds Christian literature, Cardinal Ximenes casting five thousand Korans into the fire, Olaus, King of Sweden, committing the Runic books to the flames, and Puritans destroying every work they could find that had about it a vestige of popery — these are all, or were in their day, vandals. The world is none the worse for having outgrown their "zeal without knowledge." Literature is a sacred thing.

> "Who of us can tell
> What he had been, had Cadmus never taught
> The art that fixes into form the thought—
> Had Plato never spoken from his cell,
> Or his high harp blind Homer never strung."

8   The Companionship of Books

What delight can be compared with an evening in the society of good books, in a quiet little study hidden away from the noisy world? Over the library at Alexandria was inscribed: "Treasury of Remedies for the Mind," and Greek students were in the habit of calling their books, "Medicine for the Soul." What healing properties are contained between the covers of old folios, and what delicious elixirs and cordials flow down the heights of literature, and fall into the weary and fainting soul to revive its energies and renew its hopes! Words can never adequately describe the ardent affection a man of letters feels for his books, and the deep and abiding delight he derives from their society. They are companionship in solitude, consolation in affliction, compensation in misfortune, youth in old age, and peaceful courage upon the borders of the grave. Let me write over my library, " Mash Allah," —the Gift of God,—for I can say with St. Francis de Sales, "I have sought repose everywhere, and have found it only in a little corner with a little book." Did you ever consider what a wonderful and beautiful thing a great book is? In its five hundred pages may live five thousand years, crowded with the priceless wisdom of the ages. Did you think that death had overtaken the prophets of Israel, the seers and religious teachers of India, and the poets and philosophers of Greece? Turn those five hundred pages, and Isaiah, Buddha, and Homer advance to meet you, as came forth the great poets to salute Virgil and Dante in the limbo of the unbaptized. Herodotus, Sophocles, Cicero, Pindar, and the men who glorified with their genius the lands of Persia and of the far East, were never more alive than they are to-day. Once they were mortal and their bodies were racked with pain, but now they have put on immortality. Once they suffered poverty and neglect, but now they are crowned with deathless honor. They have escaped from the dust and have entered the golden realm of literature. Socrates and Aristotle no longer face the poisoned cup; Anaxagoras is never again to be dragged to a loathsome prison; Cornelius Agrippa need hide no more from malicious foes; Galileo shall be no longer as Milton found him, "poor and old"; Spenser's troubles are ended; Camoens is now freed from his bed of anguish in the Lisbon hospital; Xylander shall never again be forced to sell the most valuable of his manuscripts for a miserable dinner—all these, liberated from the sorrows and ill usages of a hard and cruel life, are now bright and blessed presences in the wonder-world of literature.

When the evening lamps are lighted, the curtains drawn, and the warm glow of the hearth-fire invites the weary soul to withdraw itself for a time from the anxiety and discord of the outer world, there come to us from the open leaves of noble books, such as Charles Lamb used to kiss with the tenderness of a lover, the ones "whom to name were to praise." They throng around us, and in their delightful society we soon lose the burdens that have pressed heavily all the long day; and out of a heart full to overflowing we exclaim with Fletcher:

> " That place that does
> Contain my books, the best companions, is
> To me a glorious court, where hourly I
> Converse with the old sages and philosophers."

Books are now so easily obtained, and for so little money, that even the most impecunious can have a choice library. Indeed, reading is the cheapest as well as the most profitable of all entertainments. Many centuries ago Solomon wrote: "Of making many books there is no end," but that wise king's knowledge of literature was confined to cumbrous rolls of papyrus or parchment, while we have hundreds of steam printing-presses throwing off from twenty thousand to thirty thousand sheets an hour, and working all the time, day and night.

In Allibone's *Dictionary of Authors*, it is stated that up to 1870 there had been published in the English language six hundred and fifty thousand different books. The author assumes that a man can read one hundred average pages a day, and that if he were to do so without missing once in the entire year, he would read in the twelve months one hundred average books. To read all the books printed in the English language up to the year 1870 would, therefore, require a life six thousand five hundred years long. But Louis XVI. read, during five months and seven days of imprisonment, one hundred and fifty-seven volumes, or one a day; and it has been said, though we may, I think, doubt the truth of the saying, that Madame de Staël-Holstein read, before she reached her fifteenth year, six hundred novels in three months, or more than six a day. The rapid multiplication of books, magazines, and papers brings with it the peril of superficiality. It requires something more than reading to make one wise. The advantage derived from the perusal of a book will depend both upon the quality of the work and the character of the reader. Bacon tells us that "Some books are to be tasted, others to be swallowed, and some few to be

chewed and digested," but where there are so
many books—good, bad, and indifferent—is it
not the part of wisdom to choose first of all the
few works worthy of being chewed and digested?
After a substantial dinner of nutritious food
we may indulge in ice-cream and confectionery,
but when these precede the dinner the appetite
for solid material is destroyed. We must cul-
tivate a manly taste for wholesome food, in
the mind as well as in the physical nature.
The books which accomplish the most good
and finally yield the greatest pleasure do not
always at first furnish the most agreeable companionship.

Theodore Parker, who was acquainted with
many books in different languages, said:
"Those books which help you most are those
which make you think the most. The hardest
way of learning is by easy reading." Let no
one fear too narrow a selection in the choosing
of books; the greatest writers and teachers
have been men of few books. What is too
widely diffused is soon wasted. Sir William
Jones never failed of reading from cover to
cover every year the works of Cicero. He
neglected many books for his Latin master,
but was not his mind well furnished, and are
not we greatly indebted to his genius and
scholarship? Fénelon lived in the society of

Homer. Malherbe could never be without his
Horace. Voltaire delighted in Racine and
Massillon. Sir William Jones, Fénelon, Malherbe, and many other writers and scholars
who chose to dwell long in the charming society
of a single book, went back for companionship
to ancient literature. The old books are often
the best. They have endured the test of time.
Thought and study have enriched their pages.
Comment and criticism have drawn to the surface all their deep meaning. Many new works
that come before the reading world with great
flourish of trumpets and blaze of glory shine
only in light borrowed from more ancient lu-
minaries. It is well for us to take Emerson's
advice and "read no mean books. Good travel-
lers stop at the best hotels; there is the best
company and the best information. In like
manner the scholar knows that the famed books
contain, first and last, the best thoughts."
And yet it must be remembered that many of
"the famed books" were once in undeserved
obscurity, and had to make a long fight for
recognition and appreciation. The mere fact
that a book is new or uncelebrated is far from
being conclusive evidence of its inferiority.
Most men are slow to recognize real merit in
humble habiliments. We too easily follow the
crowd, and without thought crown the idol of

the hour while we neglect with gross injustice the rising genius. He is wise and full of discernment who can discover the prince under a beggar's rags.

To appreciate the vastness of literature one should wander through the Congressional Library at Washington, or study Allibone's *Dictionary of Authors.* Dr. Allibone's book, without the supplement, contains notices of forty-three thousand one hundred and forty-four authors, covering three thousand three hundred pages. There are among them seven hundred Smiths, of whom ninety-two are named John. The manuscript, as copied for the press by Mrs. Allibone, consumed nineteen thousand and forty-four foolscap pages. The Congressional Library has doubled three times in fifteen years, and will soon have a million volumes. The nucleus of it all was Thomas Jefferson's library, bought for seven thousand dollars. The British Museum already counts upon its shelves a million printed books; and the Bibliothèque Nationale, of Paris, contains more than three times that number.

Let it be remembered for the encouragement of all true lovers of books, that the largest library is not the best. There is much miserable trash in the Congressional Library; and in the British Museum are many worm-eaten

manuscripts that never did and never will deserve publication. Bibliomania and genuine
love of literature are not the same thing. He
who most delights in good books is likely to
be very discriminating in his selection of works.
A man may have a passion for the accumula-
tion of books who has no real enjoyment in the
books themselves. Acquisitiveness is the same
thing in the world of printed leaves and in that
of minted gold. I knew of a man who collected
a large library, and was himself so ignorant that
it was with difficulty he could read the title-
page of any one of the thousands of books upon
his shelves. Bruyer, describing such a biblio-
maniac, wrote:

"As soon as I enter his house I am ready to
faint on the staircase from a strong smell of mo-
rocco leather; in vain he shows me fine editions,
gold leaves, and Etruscan bindings, naming them
one after another as if he were showing a gallery
of pictures! a gallery by the way he seldom tra-
verses when alone, for he rarely reads, but me he
offers to conduct through it! I thank him for his
politeness, and, as little as himself, care to visit the
tan-house which he calls his library."

Melanchthon's library at one time contained
only "the four famous P's "—Plato, Pliny,
Plutarch, and Ptolemy the geographer, but it

was the working library of a great and good man. He who possesses the Bible, Homer, and Shakespeare has a collection of books of which he need not be ashamed. A New England lecturer thinks he could make a magnificent religious library from the writings of but six authors; he would select: (1) Jeremy Taylor's *Holy Living and Holy Dying;* (2) Thomas à Kempis's *Imitation of Christ;* (3) Bunyan's *Pilgrim's Progress* and *Holy War;* (4) Pascal's *Thoughts on Religion;* (5) Horace Bushnell's *Sermons for the New Life* and *Nature and the Supernatural;* (6) Huntington's *Christian Believing and Living.*

Into every life, be it long or short, there must enter dark and lonely days when the soul earnestly desires to escape from the surrounding world, and longs for some quiet and restful companionship; next to religion, literature furnishes the society such seasons demand. Books are the sweet and uncomplaining companions of solitary hours. They forsake us not when old age arrives; indeed they furnish a most delightful solace for the fatigues and disabilities of "three-score-and-ten." As we increase in years we naturally contract the circle of our reading, until at last the old man's intellectual life is all contained between the covers of that one book which, while it is the

guide of youth, is also the staff of old age; and
he finds it literally true as Whittier sings:

> " We search the world for truth, we cull
> The good, the pure, the beautiful
> From graven stone and written scroll,
> From the old flower-fields of the soul;
> And, weary seekers for the best,
> We come back laden from our quest,
> To find that all the sages said
> Is in the book our mothers read."

In this great world so full of tears and
laughter, and all manner of change, with infinite variety of feeling and taste—this world
where wisdom and folly must not only stop at
the same inn, but even lie down together in
the same bed, are hundreds of men and women
who have the audacity to call themselves educated, and even cultivated, and who yet always
think of books as *things*. These regard the
universal genius and rich beauty and fas-
cination of Homer and Shakespeare as mere
marketable commodities, to be had in various
conditions of internal and external adornment
for from a dime to many dollars. To their
view, books are furniture, often ornamental
and sometimes necessary, in the same way that
dining-room tables and comfortable chairs are
essential to civilized life. A fellowship of

hat-racks and umbrella-stands would be quite
as intelligible to them as a fellowship of books.
If by some cruel trick of ill-fortune this page
should come under the eye of any such Philistine, I beg him, with my best bow and sweetest
smile, to put aside, without parley or hesitation,
what was not intended for his perusal, and to
leave the author to find his readers among men
and women who are so utterly crazy as to love
books for their own sakes.

When, refreshed by quiet sleep, I leave my
chamber, and, in the morning, descend for
coffee and rolls, what a blessed company of
old friends, with here and there a newcomer,
shy and modest, and yet glad to be where I am
glad to have him, await my presence with the
salutation of all lands and ages. Only a few
days ago there came to my library from a
Philadelphia bookseller, whom may Heaven
bless, Seilhamer's *History of the American
Theatre*, Delafield's *Inquiry into the Origin of
the Antiquities of America* (a fine old copy,
with the long plate in perfect condition), and
a curious old book containing the poems of
George Peele (1552–1598), one of the city poets
of London. What a sorry lot of rhymers
and inventors of doggerel were those sons of
song, appointed so long ago to celebrate the
good qualities of the old London mayors, and

to dignify the municipal authorities of the great English capital!

It is customary to deride the memory of George Peele, and, in fact, it is hard to find even an erudite who has made himself acquainted with more than a page or two of his laborious work. But in reality the old writer was not so bad a fellow after all. It is true we know of his personal appearance from this somewhat unattractive description: "A handsome person with a thin womanish voice; of light and nimble fancy, and smooth, ingenious execution; without the faintest desire to use honest means in procuring a livelihood." It is true that he was something of a "tramp," and did not regulate his life by any known and approved standard of morality. It is also true that he did not see the world, such as it was in his day, through the eyes of James Russell Lowell. He may have been one of the most pronounced of vagabonds; and somewhat less inclined to a silk hat and evening-suit than was ever our own dear old Walt Whitman. But somehow I think he was not so bad a fellow after all, nor quite so lazy as it is orthodox to believe. He numbered among his friends the "thousand-souled" Shakespeare and "rare Ben Jonson." He could not have been so very idle, for he composed five plays, several pastorals, and a number of minor poems and epigrams. His *Edward I.* is well worth reading, which is more than can be said of most of the poems of the present English laureate. Milton browsed on the fat pasture-land of his *Old Wives' Tale*, else how could the great Puritan have given us *Comus ?* And his *Love of King David and the Fair Bethsabe* is good for the literature of any age. Yes, I am indeed glad that my heavenly bookseller in Philadelphia sent me the poems of George Peele. That bookseller will retain his celestial standing in my fancy notwithstanding the sinister fact that he extracted from my pocket two dollars more than was his due.

The earliest of the city poets was John Heywood. I do not know that he was any more inclined to the sober side of life than was our friend Peele. He had a fine time at the court of Henry VIII., where he was musician, wit, and play-writer. The only thing he ever wrote that any one cares for in these days is *The Four P's*, and I am not sure that any one cares very much for that. Yet it has in it some quotable lines, and can be read if one will make the effort, which is more than can be said of anything Anthony Munday, a later city poet, ever produced. I have in my library, not far from the works of Heywood, *The White*

Devil, which John Webster made. He made also *The Devil's Law Case.* He was fond of the Devil, and, if we may trust history, the Devil was not wholly averse to him.

Who does not like Ben Jonson, bricklayer, soldier, actor, poet-laureate, and theatrical writer and critic? He was a man of prodigious intellectual force, though not so well provided with ideality as we could wish. His name is forever associated with the most exquisite lyric in the English language—*To Celia.* It was a sour day for "rare Ben" when Cumberland discovered that the lovely poem was not original, but translated from Philostratus, who flourished so long ago that perhaps his ownership in the poem is not worth considering. In some ways, Jonson's lines are an improvement upon those of his classic predecessor. Was Jonson a plagiarist? Now, reader, consider the force and scope of that question. Do you know of any really good writer who is not to some extent a plagiarist? Where were Shakespeare if a man might not borrow without troubling himself to say anything about it? There are iconoclasts (Heaven have mercy on their conventional souls!) who hint that Dante's *Inferno* is derived from *The Visions of Alberico,* and that *Paradise Lost* is not lost to us, simply because of the Anglo-Saxon of Cædmon. The learned Dunlop studied the novels of Europe with great care, and found that they contained about three hundred distinct stories, two hundred of which could be traced to centuries before Christ, and to the other side of the Black Sea. Two hundred years before *The Psalm of Life* appeared in the *Knickerbocker Magazine*, Henry King, Bishop of Chichester, expressed himself thus:

> " But hark! my Pulse, like soft drum,
>   Beats my approach, tells thee I come;
>   And slow howe'er my marches be,
>   I shall at last sit down with thee."

Yes, we owe much to the noble army of plagiarists. I think we all know of writers who would be far greater in the Kingdom of Letters were they less original.

I envy not the man who loves not books. Books are friends to win our confidence and cheer our lonely hours. They are not *things* of commercial value only, nor are they treasures to hide away and hoard. They are friends and companions of the well-filled pipe, the mug of ale, and the rainy day.

SOME TREASURES OF AN AUTO-
GRAPH COLLECTOR

OLD letters are a peculiarly interesting kind of literature. Here is a package of epistles some of which were written many years before their present owner drew the breath of life. They have extended their existence through generations of autograph-lovers, to rest at last in the little drawer that holds in quiet seclusion a few sacred mementos of the long ago. I did not intend to open the package this evening, but the string that confined the creased and yellow pages was brittle from age, and fell apart.

Here is a curious epistle in the handwriting of Mercier, who translated Zimmermann's *Solitude* into French. Its three pages chronicle a sorrow that had long shadowed his life, but which in the letter is described so vaguely that I cannot be entirely sure of its nature. Mercier tells his correspondent that Zimmermann opened to him a new world and gave him his first real delight in nature. He enlarges

upon his weariness of Paris, and thinks of
seeking a home upon some inaccessible island.
At the end of the letter, just under the signature, some unknown hand has traced in pencil lines a French couplet, which I venture
to translate thus:

" Hast thou a sorrow? In no human heart confide;
But far away, with Nature, evermore abide."

Here is a letter from a gentleman of the
olden time.   He remembers the completion of
the Erie Canal, October 26, 1825, and how,
when the last workman threw down his tools at
Buffalo, the news was conveyed from that city
to New York by the discharge of cannon in
just one hour and thirty minutes.   There was
a cannon stationed every ten miles of the
distance, and over that great chain, three hundred miles long, there rolled a continuous
thunder of glad triumph.   But the completion
of the canal failed of infusing into the old
gentleman a progressive spirit, for in this very
letter, which bears date of May 25, 1833, we
find him denouncing the little railroad that ran
into Schenectady as "a most dangerous con-
trivance."   He congratulates himself and the
good friend to whom the letter is addressed
that "it is quite unlikely any more railroad

experiments will ever be made." He much prefers the Thorps and Sprague stages, and thinks them marvels of convenience and luxury. He also recommends the coaches of Parker & Co., of Utica, and has a good word for the Cleveland stages that start from Rochester.

Here is another letter. It is dated January 12, 1826, and bears the signature of no less a man than the Hon. Stephen Allen of New York. To whom the letter is addressed does not appear, for the obvious reason that some barbarian has cut off a portion of the first page. The subject under consideration is penitentiary discipline. The letter describes solitary confinement as "a punishment much in favor with many, but capable of great abuse." Mr. Allen is sure that Pennsylvania is not inhuman in its treatment of criminals, as has been charged (so he intimates) by certain English reformers. How Mr. Allen comes to know so much about Pennsylvania is easily understood when we find him recommending certain opinions expressed by Robert Vaux, who was in his day a famous citizen of old Philadelphia. The letter has some sharp things to say of a Mr. Roscoe (I suppose the author of the delightful books about Lorenzo de' Medici and Leo X.), who is pushing " a sentimental philanthropy" quite too far. The letter is valuable as showing how even in those days the questions that now agitate the mind of Mr. Round of the Prison Association, and engross the attention of the good men and women who work with him, stirred the thoughts and moved the pens of well-wishers of their kind.

Here is still another letter daintily written by a lady of colonial times, who has succeeded in hiding her identity behind the initials E. B. The happy youth (for young, brave, and handsome I must believe him to have been) had no other name than George for this fair correspondent.   E. B. and George—we shall never know more of these lovers, read between the lines as industriously and as sympathetically as we may.

> " Who wrote those tender words of love
>   Long years ago?
>   The grave holds well that secret now,
>   'Neath flowers and snow."

Here is a letter from Mrs. Hemans complaining to the publisher of the *New Monthly* that her "Landing of the Pilgrim Fathers" had suffered a sea-change in his periodical. "And the sounding aisles of the dim woods rang" has made a journey into the far country of prose, and "the sounding aisles" are now most

shamefully metamorphosed into "the *surrounding* aisles." The mistake must certainly have
grieved the gifted authoress, but her letter is
kind and womanly, and even in some degree
apologetic.

Here is still another letter. It bears the
signature of one whom every lover of the
beautiful delights to honor:

" NEW YORK, Feb. 3, 1848.

"COL. J. G. TOTTEN.

" *My dear Sir*,—Conely has promised to forward
to you to-day the picture of Faith. I do not know
by what express (Conely has, since I commenced,
been here, and says the picture was sent this morning by Adams Express). I should be glad if the
painting pleases you as well as it has some of my
kind and partial Brooklyn admirers. I took the
liberty of sending it (while drying) to Pierpont
street, where it was visited by many, and seemed
to produce some effect among the ladies. The
subject has interested me deeply, and I have painted
it *heartily*,—more so than any work I have at-
tempted for years, which has made me resolve not
to sell myself any longer, and be laboring at subjects in which I feel but slight interest. The
reason of Faith being clothed in white, with a
cross of bloody tinge on her bosom and wearing
for an ornament the words written on the border,
will be at once apparent. I have also introduced

light in three colored rays to symbolize the trinity,
that holy mystery which I must regard as the test
of a true and unhesitating faith.   There is a reason
for the order in which the colors are arranged in
the trio which will perhaps be thought fanciful.
Red is assumed, as representative of our Saviour,
of course indicating the bloody sacrifice.   Blue, of
the eternal Father, as expressive of infinite space,
distance, irresistibility, and perfect serenity.   Yellow I have adopted for the Holy Spirit, as being
the color of warmth,— the cheering, life-giving,
and fructifying principle of light.   To be seen to
advantage, the picture should be hung considerably
above the eye, as the foreshortening supposes a
low point of sight.

"Please give my best regards to the ladies of
your family.   I regret that I shall not be able to see
them in Washington this winter, but I am obliged
reluctantly to give up the idea of leaving town for
some months yet.   With great regard and respect,
"Most truly yours,
"D. HUNTINGTON."

I have a delightful letter, four pages long, in
the handwriting of George Crabbe, surgeon,
clergyman, and "poet of the poor"; a man of
noblest spirit and the kindest heart; every
where known in his day as "the gentleman
with the sour name and the sweet countenance."   Crabbe's long and familiar letter is

addressed to a Mr. Waldron, and recounts with evident satisfaction his experience at a breakfast with Mr. Brougham and Lady Holland; after which he attended, with Lord Holland, the dinner at Freemason's Tavern, upon the occasion of Kemble's retiring. The gentleman from whom I obtained the letter purchased it, and another which the poet wrote about the same time, at a sale of literary material in London. The other letter was burned by an ignorant servant, who supposed, from its faded and creased condition, that it had no value. An ignoramus in a library is like a bull in a china-shop, and calls for something more vigorous than protest. Many books and manuscripts of the greatest importance have been lost to the world through the rude ignorance of men incapable of appreciating their value, and who accounted them to be rubbish. Old Captain Woodes Rogers, who, more than a century ago, overhauled the Spanish brig *Marquess*, has left an excellent reputation for nautical skill and unflinching courage, but he was a wild and dangerous iconoclast in the realm of letters. He found with other cargo five hundred bales of papal indulgences, sixteen reams in a bale, stowed away in the hold of the Spanish brig. He says in his report, which, because it did not fall into the hand of an iconoclast like himself, has been preserved:

"These indulgences were consigned to South American priests, who were directed to retail them at prices varying from fifty pesos down to three reales, according to purchaser's rank, wealth, and moral condition.   I could not see that they were of any value, and so threw them all overboard, with the exception of a few that I kept to burn the pitch off the ships' bottoms when we wanted to careen them."

Doubtless the world is not seriously damaged by the loss of the five hundred bales of papal indulgences that the fish obtained for nothing, but it chills one to the heart to reflect that, had those bales been original drafts of the *Iliad* in the actual handwriting of Homer, the fish could have had them at as little cost.

STEVENSON AND FATHER DAMIEN

THE Rev. Dr. Charles McEwen Hyde, while in this country, just after the Stevenson episode, spent an entire morning with me, in my study, at Great Barrington, Massachusetts, where at the time I was pastor of the First Congregational Church. He gave me the entire story of Stevenson's brutal letter, and the controversy that ensued, from first to last. I asked him many questions, all of which he answered promptly and at length. I rose from that interview absolutely certain in my mind that everything Dr. Hyde had said of Damien in his letter to the Rev. H. B. Gage (published in *The Sydney Presbyterian* for October 26, 1889) was true. Through the entire conversation, Dr. Hyde spoke in the spirit of kindness and Christian charity of both Damien and Stevenson, and I discovered in all that he had to say nothing bearing the slightest approach to a bitter or vindictive temper. Whether it was wise at the time and under the circumstances to write the letter he addressed to Mr.

Gage is another question, and one I am not competent to answer. Dr. Hyde wrote the letter from a sense of duty, and never, so far as I know, did he regret the sending of it, or wish that its statements had been in any wise different. Stevenson's letter was, I am fully persuaded, more the work of the rhetorician than of the man. He was carried away by the opportunity of making a rhetorical flourish and impression, and so went farther than he intended to go, and much farther than his own judgment approved. I think he regretted the letter, and would have been glad to recall it had recall been possible. I also think that had he lived he would have made some kind of an apology. Stevenson was a man of many noble qualities, and conscience was not wanting as an element of power in his life, but his letter to Dr. Hyde was not honest, nor had it for any great length of time the approval of his own inner sense of right and justice. He did not really believe what he wrote, neither did he intend to write what he did. The temptation from a literary point of view was great, and the writer got the better of the man.

I do not intend to say that Stevenson was an actual hypocrite, for he undoubtedly worked himself up into some kind of self-approval. It

is certainly not a difficult thing for a man of
ardent imagination to fancy himself convinced
of what in his heart of hearts he knows to be
without foundation in fact. There are in history many illustrations of the wonderful power
of the human mind to deliberately deceive
itself in the interest of its own inclinations.
It was by no means admiration for Damien that
led to Stevenson's onslaught upon a good man
and a veteran missionary; it was the power of
a bewitching literary opportunity which he had
not the strength of character to resist. One
of his letters since published (*Stevenson's Letters*, vol. ii., p. 188), makes what I am saying
clear enough. These are his words:

"Of old Damien, whose weaknesses and worse
perhaps I heard fully, I think only the more. He
was a European peasant; dirty, bigoted, untruthful,
unwise, tricky, but superb with generosity, residual
candour, and fundamental good humour; convince
him he had done wrong (it might take hours of in-
sult) and he would undo what he had done, and
like his corrector better. A man with all the grime
and paltriness of mankind, but a saint and hero all
the more for that."

Those words are nothing but an endeavor on
Stevenson's part to compromise by resaying
and unsaying at the same time what he was
3

conscious he should never have said. How
could a man of his mental qualities and training believe that one distinguished for his "untruthful and tricky" character could be at the
same time "superb with residual candour"?
How could he account Damien all the more a
saint and hero because of his "grime and paltriness"? Stevenson did not think the leper
priest a great saint, nor did he hold him in his
heart to be a hero. He knew better from the
first, and his own letter convicts him of a gross
lack of candor.

Stevenson drifted from his early religious
moorings, and Dr. Hyde, in his conversation
with me at my home in Great Barrington,
seemed to think that the violence of his attack
was in some measure due to spiritual unrest;
and to a feeling of resentment against the
creed of his youth, which, with all his effort,
he never succeeded in wholly renouncing.
There is abundant evidence that during the
latter part of his life he was religiously uncertain. His early training came to his help time
and time again, and he did not know what it
was that helped him. To the very orthodoxy
which he impugned he clung for spiritual life.

John Burroughs wrote in his *The Light of
Day*, which many readers will account to be
nothing more than a very dim sort of twilight:

"How impossible for me to read the Bible as father and Jerry did, or to feel any interest in questions which were vital to them."

But Stevenson, with all his parade of superior intelligence, never could get away from his religious past. It haunted him day and night, and everywhere in his more serious writings are the unmistakable symptoms of uncertainty and misgiving. He was more or less of a believer in the old-time orthodoxy, and that directly in the face of his own will. "Jekyll and Hyde" were in his own heart, and the conflict spoiled his temper. The self-contradictions and unreasonableness of the Damien letter all reflect the unrest of the author. Could a calm and quiet mind, especially in a man so well trained and so intelligent as was Robert Louis Stevenson, exalt over the clean and orderly home of a missionary, "the pig-sty" in which he declares he found the leper priest?

Stevenson's description of Damien negatives all the praise he has bestowed upon him—these are his words:

"A man of the peasant class, certainly of the peasant type, shrewd, ignorant, bigoted, rough in his ways, indiscreet, officious, domineering, unpopular with the Kanakas, with a mania for doctoring, with slovenly ways and false ideas of hygiene, adhering to his errors with perfect obstinacy."

Out of such material, what kind of a saint and hero can you make? Dr. Hyde insisted, and I have no doubt his statement was true, that the death of Damien was not due to leprosy, though he was a leper at the time of his death. It was caused by pneumonia, for which he would not take the medicines his physician prescribed, though he was urged to do so. That he was a devout Roman Catholic and loved his Church, no one will deny. That he did some hard work and performed some kind deeds is also freely admitted. But that he was a clean, intelligent, and pure-minded man, who lived and died for others, no sane person, who knows of what he writes, can for a moment believe. Edward Clifford may have thought Damien a saint and a hero, for he knew nothing about the matter one way or the other, and his book is a bit of sentimentalism and literary gush, but Stevenson did know about the leper priest, and he could not have been honest at heart when he wrote his letter to Dr. Hyde.

The frequent reprinting of the Damien letter is due entirely to its brilliant rhetorical artillery fire. It contains nothing that recommends it to the good judgment and kind feelings of any man. It carries no conviction of truth. It is brutal, violent, and unreasonable.

Even were all its charges sustained, still its
spirit would be unworthy of a calm and charitable mind.   Over against Mr. Stevenson's fine
writing I place Dr. Hyde's faithful services in
two American churches before he went to
Honolulu, and his work for nearly a quarter
of a century in a missionary enterprise which
has transformed the Hawaiian Islands.   That
those who were upon the field and knew by
personal observation and experience what was
the truth in the controversy, continued to
honor Dr. Hyde with their confidence up to
the last day of his useful life, shows conclu-
sively that at Honolulu the Damien letter was
never regarded as anything more than a striking exhibition of literary pyrotechny.

MODERN BUILDERS OF AIR-CASTLES

THE sale of the old "Nashabah" estate, near Memphis, reminds us of the brilliant and eccentric career of the accomplished and elegant Frances Wright, who purchased that property in 1825 under the impression that it was a good place to commence the experiment of educating negroes. Frances was left an orphan at the age of nine years, and with her sister Sylvia was heir to a large estate. It was the misfortune of both children that they were wards of a philosopher, who had determined in his erudite mind to make them subjects of philosophic experimentation, and to bring them up in accordance with his own idea of what a woman should be. Frances was as unlike any other woman as Jeremy Bentham could make her. She was of a nature strange and meteoric, but old Bentham intensified her peculiarities and made her even more impracticable than she would otherwise have been. The philosopher did not realize his ideal of womanly excellence in the beautiful and astonishing creature

38

his training gave to the world. He wished to
make of her a great scholar of his own type,
but her mind was too mercurial for deep and
continuous thought, and her heart too warm
and womanly for metaphysical abstractions.
He destroyed the influence of her Presbyterian
birth, but he never eradicated extravagant
fondness for the refinements and luxuries of
polite life. And yet close friendship always
united guardian and ward, and Frances dedicated her second book, *A Few Days in Athens*,
which was published in 1822, to Jeremy Bentham. Bentham himself seems to have enjoyed
the pleasures of this life with a keenness not always associated with philosophic temperament
and pursuits. He succeeded to his father's
property, and had money enough to live in
London and employ a number of young men
as secretaries. He was not extravagant, nor,
as a general rule, over self-indulgent, but he
always avoided whatever was calculated to occasion discomfort, and when he firmly believed
that his last hour was near, he said to one
of his disciples who was watching over him, "I
now feel that I am dying. Our care must be
to minimize the pain." Mirabeau seems to
have viewed his departure out of this life in
the same light: "My friend, I shall die to-day.
Now that I am in this situation there remain

but one thing more for you to do, and that is to perfume me, to crown me with flowers, to environ me with music." That Frances became a materialist is not strange, but that she was so far from a sensualist and so much of a philanthropist is wonderful indeed. Hers was what Frances Power Cobbe calls "a magnanimous atheism." She was pure and generous without the hope of a life to come. She worked for others without any of the ordinary incentives of piety. She was supported by an enthusiasm for humanity, and to her virtue (there being no future state) was its own reward. Her absorbing idea was to make our stupid and money-getting world over after the community pattern, and to that end she charmed society with her eloquence, for she was much more of an orator in her day than was Anna Dickenson in ours. She was flattered and admired, and "Fanny Wright Societies" were organized in nearly all of the Atlantic States. She was denounced by the pulpit and applauded by the press—both by calling attention to her peculiar views advertised her lectures. Her beauty, culture, and eloquence took men by storm. But it all ended in smoke —the fragrant smoke of costly incense from a silver censer, but smoke after all, and nothing but smoke. So ended Robert Owen's scheme and the Brookfarm arrangement; so will end the marvellous revelations of the Fox sisters and of Andrew Jackson Davis; and so will fall in glittering ruins in the years to come many another castle in the air. Michael Angelo, it is said, was once commanded by Pietro de' Medici to mould a statue out of snow; and so are gifted men and women to-day commanded by their own undisciplined minds to build castles in the air more unsubstantial than "the baseless fabric of a vision." It is sad to contemplate the amount of genuine ability constantly withdrawn from worthy channels by the foolish conceits of unbalanced intellects.

I once knew a man of rare learning and great goodness of heart who spent the best portion of his life in the effort to discover a method of so illuminating the human body as to render visible to the unassisted eye of the physician all the internal organs. "When my great discovery is perfected," said the enthusiast to me, "man's intestines will be as transparent as glass, and by inclining the head upon the breast one may without difficulty gaze into his own stomach." He once disclosed to me the origin of his prospective discovery—I excerpt his statement from my note-book:

" Dr. Richardson, of London, while experimenting with electricity illuminated two of his fingers so

that they were perfectly transparent. Quite re-
cently, Dr. Thomas Nicholson, of New Orleans,
succeeded in illuminating his entire hand. His
experiment was conducted with a powerful incandescent light from an oxyhydrogen blowpipe and
large magnifying lenses. Dr. Nicholson's success
is at best only a clumsy hint of what is possible. I
shall use no external apparatus, but shall render
the human body self-luminous by the application
of a peculiar ointment the constituents of which I
am not yet prepared to disclose."

Nothing could induce the man to turn his attention in another direction. Failure only increased his zeal. He would cite the case of
Bernard Palissy, who, after working sixteen
years, and burning all the furniture in his
house, came off victorious, and answered the
laughter of his neighbors and the reproaches
of his wife with beautiful enamel. "My discovery," said he, "will be greater than that of
the famous French potter." And so year after year he went on

" Dropping buckets into empty wells,
    And growing old in drawing nothing up."

The gifted Sylvia Wright followed her sister
Frances to America, and bought a tract of
land, with which she hoped to save a foolish

world that cared nothing about being saved.
Her story is at once sad and ludicrous. Upon
a cold winter night she was informed that her
head farmer was dangerously ill with fever.
Her womanly heart was touched, and she
nursed him faithfully until he recovered. He
was a handsome fellow, but coarse and brutal.
His manners were bad and his morals worse.
He was a great animal in human form. Notwithstanding all this the beautiful and cultivated Sylvia fell wildly in love with the ass-
headed Bottom and married him. The dream
was delightful while it lasted, but at the end
of two months it dissolved in a mist of pain,
and the gentle Titania loathed the miserable and ignorant Bottom, who had not the
decency to treat her with ordinary humanity,
but kicked her about the house just as it was
afterward discovered he had been in the habit
of kicking her cattle about the barnyard.
Sylvia fled to Europe and soon died from
mortification, leaving a daughter to the care
of Frances. Thus ended Sylvia's effort to
reform the world. It is very unprofitable
work, this search for perpetual motion and
the Greek Kalends, and yet, strange to say,
it possesses peculiar charm for a certain class
of minds. The man in Scripture who built
his house upon the sand has a multitude of

imitators who learn nothing from the experience of others.

Frances Wright married a Frenchman named d'Arusmont, from whom she was compelled to separate. She adopted her sister's child, calling it Sylvia d'Arusmont. The girl inherited a large fortune from both mother and aunt, but, alas, the wild romantic flame burned in her veins and kept her blood at the boiling point. She employed a miserable wretch, Eugene Picault, as her agent in America, and he stole her heart as the first step toward stealing her property. In order to marry Sylvia and possess himself of her money, he abandoned his wife and children. The guilty ones changed their names to La Guthrie, and lived together many years, leaving three children, who, after the death of their parents, were adjudged bastards.

Another architect of air-castles was the amateur philosopher, John Cleves Symmes, the once famous author of the theory of concentric spheres. He held that the earth was hollow, and that within our globe were wonderlands where roamed strange animals, grew marvellous flowers, and dwelt mighty races of human beings. To read his lectures was very much like reading *The Arabian Nights*. He regarded himself as a new Columbus; and urged the government to sail through the icy circle around the pole, and so enter the enchanted country he had brought to light. "Symmes's Hole" created a great deal of merriment, but its discoverer and defender never lost heart. He spent much money and gave all his time to the new theory. He bore reproach and ridicule without a murmur, and with his dying breath insisted upon the concentric spheres, and the Arctic hole through which a ship might sail from an open polar sea into the very interior of our globe. The author of the theory of concentric spheres believed that there was no ice within five hundred miles of the pole, and that at the pole the temperature was that of the torrid zone. During his life he made a few converts who paid part of his expenses and published his manuscripts, and it is said that there are to-day some who still hold to his peculiar theory of the construction of our planet. Poor Symmes built his castle in the air, and without any real philosophical attainment thought to make over the wisdom of the ages after the crude and fanciful conceptions of his own disordered mind. "Symmes's Hole" and "The Nashabah Estate" are ruins more eloquent than those of Baalbek, for they mark the failure of noble purpose, disinterested benevolence, and self-sacrificing toil.

The Brookfarm movement received the active
support and co-operation of the most cultivated
men and women in the New England of half a
century ago.   Among its friends and patrons
were George Ripley, Charles Dana, George
W. Curtis, Theodore Parker, Ralph Waldo
Emerson, William Henry Channing, Nathaniel
Hawthorne, A. Bronson Alcott, Elizabeth Pea-
body, Margaret Fuller, and besides these
"many ladies, whom to name were to praise."
Not all of these divine ones lived at the farm,
but they all encouraged the movement and
identified themselves to some extent with its
history.   Brookfarm resulted from a very curious state of affairs in New England.   Massachusetts was the hot-bed of all kinds of reforms
and reformers, and T. W. Higginson counted
"eighty-two pestilent heresies" in that single
State.   The philosophical and social heavens
were full of new and strange stars—stars that
declined classification and refused fixed orbits.
Old constellations were falling asunder, and
from coruscations and signs and wonders one
might have concluded that the moral heavens
were about to be rolled together as a scroll.
Brownson was preaching German metaphysics,
and Parker was rationalizing theology.   Edward
Palmer had just announced the "No-money
Gospel," and was industriously persuading the

impecunious that the love of money is the root
of all evil. Graham was fulminating against
bolted flour. Phrenology had placed its divin-
ing hand upon every man's skull. Anti-slavery
agitation was coming to the front, and the
famous Hutchinson family were singing for
freedom, and speaking for it too wherever
opportunity presented itself. Alcott, who was
never anything more than a shadow of the
Sage of Concord, was on hand with his the-
ories. The woman's rights movement demanded a hearing. *The Dial* had just made
its appearance. Margaret Fuller was convers-
ing with the progressive minds of Boston. All
Massachusetts, and especially the "Hub of the
Universe," was turned upside down. The old
faiths were being unsettled, and new ones were
forming on every side. And suddenly from
out of all this seething mass of spiritual and
intellectual chaos, there came forth a creative
light never before seen in the heavens. Thus
Theodore Parker introduces the new luminary:

"The brilliant genius of Emerson rose in the
winter night and hung over Boston, drawing the
eyes of ingenuous young people to look to that
great new star, and a beauty and a mystery which
charmed for the moment, while it gave also peren-
nial instruction, as it led them forward along new
paths and toward new hopes."

This ferment was not confined to the upper classes, but had worked its way into the hearts of common people. Farmers and factory-hands were disposing of problems that had puzzled Plato and utterly routed the Seven Wise Men of Greece. Children were not afraid to answer questions over which philosophers had pored in vain. When Higginson went to a manufacturing town in Massachusetts a youthful agitator inquired of him, "Do you know the Riggs girls who work in the mill?" On being informed that Higginson had not the honor of their acquaintance, he expressed great surprise, and said, "You ought to know them! Interested in all the reforms! Know all about temperance, anti-slavery, bathe in cold water every morning, and one of 'em 's a Grahamite." Higginson made their acquaintance upon the recommendation of the aforesaid youthful agitator, and pronounced them "exceedingly sensible and well-informed women." The story of the child who was found in front of Emerson's house digging for the "infinite" was not without many a parallel in the New England of fifty years ago. Emerson was in the habit of holding receptions in Boston. After his lecture he would retire to the room of a crude young man who seems to have been, like Ephraim, "a cake not turned," and would

there converse with those of his hearers who
desired greater light. Higginson says that this
young man, who was infatuated with the doctrines of Fourier, had placed upon the door
leading to his apartment a glaring sun having
yellow rays, with this motto in the centre:
" Universal Unity." Beneath it was painted in
plain black letters the more practical and
common-sense inscription : "Please wipe your
dirty feet!" In this young enthusiast's room
Emerson delivered to schoolgirls and intellectual boys some of his most wonderful dis-
courses. What sort of men and women it was
often Emerson's duty to address may be
gathered from his own account of "The Char-
don Street Convention." He says :

" If the assembly was disorderly, it was picturesque. Madmen, madwomen, men with beards,
Dunkers, Muggletonians, Come-outers, Groaners,
Agrarians, Seventh-day Baptists, Quakers, Abolitionists, Calvinists, Unitarians and Philosophers,
all came successively to the top, and seized their
moment, if not their hour, wherein to chide, or
pray, or preach, or protest."

Mr. Frothingham thinks all this ferment in
New England was the direct result of mighty
movements abroad, and he quotes John Morley
as saying: "A great wave of humanity, of

4

benevolence, of desire for improvement—a great wave of social sentiment, in short, poured itself among all who had the faculty of large and disinterested thinking." Mr. Frothingham instances (in his *Life of George Ripley*, page 109) the work of Dr. Pusey and of Dr. Newman; the efforts put forth by Thomas Arnold and F. D. Maurice to broaden the Church of England; the vigorous exposure of shams by Thomas Carlyle; the pictures of abuses and cruelties which were drawn by that wizard of our English language, Charles Dickens; Kingsley's outspoken and manly protest against iniquities; Cobden's agitation, and the attack upon monopolies which was being made by John Bright and Daniel O'Connell. No doubt all these forces were at work, yet much was due to the new life which was springing up in New England as a healthful reaction from the grim ethics and stilted and unnatural life of Puritanism.

From such strange and discordant elements grew the Brookfarm movement—chaotic and brilliant. The association was formed in 1841, and purchased at West Roxbury a farm of about two hundred acres, for which it paid ten thousand five hundred dollars. The farm was conveniently located near to Theodore Parker's meeting-house, and was upon the spot where

Eliot, the "Apostle to the Indians," had preached the Gospel to American savages. Mr. Ripley was the president, Charles A. Dana was the recording secretary, and Minot Pratt was the treasurer. Some of the members put in money, and others gave their labor. The following is a copy of the original paper of subscription:

"We, the undersigned, do hereby agree to pay the sum attached to our names, to be invested in the Brookfarm Institute of Agriculture and Education, according to the conditions described in the foregoing articles of association. Date, 1841.

NAMES.	SHARES.	
George Ripley............Nos.	1, 2, and 3......	$1,500
Nath. Hawthorne........... "	18 and 19.......	1,000
Minot Pratt................. "	4, 5, and 6......	1,500
Charles A. Dana............. "	10, 11, and 12...	1,500
William B. Allen............ "	7, 8, and 9......	1,500
Sophia W. Ripley........... "	16 and 17.......	1,000
Maria T. Pratt.............. "	20 and 21.......	1,000
Sarah F. Stearns............. "	22 and 23.......	1,000
Marianne Ripley............ "	13, 14, and 15...	1,500
Charles O. Whitmore........ "	24.............	500"

Every member of this delightful "Garden of Eden" did whatever was good in his or her own eyes. There were no masters. Every laborer settled for himself the question as to how many hours were to constitute a working-day. Each member chose to work or play as fancy directed. Emerson says that the country members "were surprised to observe that one man ploughed all day and one looked out of the window all day, and perhaps drew his picture, and both received at night the same wages." The surprise did not last long, for the country members soon found that "they also serve who only stand and wait." The workers at first were many, but after a short time it was hard to find a man who was willing to dig or plough, and Mr. Ripley would go every day to the barn-yard and do the dirty work as a rebuke and an example. No one took the hint, and soon the faithful president of this most hopeful enterprise added milking to his other duties. The women at their washing recited Greek poems, but as they could not wring the clothes without taking cold, the gentlemen were requested to assist. William Allen, the head-farmer, found that two of his most important field-hands had left oxen and other implements of labor in the field, and had gone off botanizing. In the morning one man said, "I will dig potatoes," and another said, "I will spend the day in studying Swedenborg." There were some in the community who eschewed the refinements of civilization, and it is reported of one man that he ate with his fingers as a protest against knives, forks, and spoons. They were accustomed to say, "It was so-and-so with us before we came out of civilization." Emerson wrote to Carlyle as follows:

" We are all a little wild here with numberless projects of social reform. Not a reading man but has a draft of a new community in his waistcoat pocket. I am gently mad myself, and am resolved to live cleanly. George Ripley is taking up a colony of agriculturists and scholars, with whom he threatens to take the field and the book. One man renounces the use of animal food; and another of coin; and on the whole we have a commendable share of reason and hope."—*Correspondence of Carlyle and Emerson*, vol. i., p. 308.

This extract does not describe the Brookfarm experiment, for Ripley's movement, here referred to, was really a "trial trip," preliminary to the West Roxbury Association, but it shows what spirits were in the air, and so gives us a genuine glimpse of Brookfarm itself. Elsewhere Emerson wrote of the reformers of Brookfarm: "They defied each other like a congress of kings, each of whom had a realm to rule, and a way of his own that made concert unprofitable." Oliver Wendell Holmes calls them an army of visionaries, and accounts for the fact that Emerson never lived at the farm by saying: "His sympathies were not allowed to mislead him; he knew human nature too well to believe in a Noah's ark full of idealists."

The life at Brookfarm was extremely simple, and had about it many hard and homely features; but it had its bright side—its superb companionships and its delightful freedom from the conventional restraints of society. The friends were very fond of each other, and did all in their power to make their "Garden of Eden" a happy and profitable home. Emerson says:

"The founders of Brookfarm have this praise, that they made what all people try to make, an agreeable place to live in. All comers, even the most fastidious, found it the pleasantest of residences. It is certain that freedom from household routine, variety of character and talent, variety of work, variety of means of thought and instruction, art, music, poetry, reading, masquerade, did not permit sluggishness or despondency; broke up routine. There is agreement in the testimony that it was, to most of the associates, education; to many, the most important period of their life, the birth of valued friendships, their first acquaintance with the riches of conversation, their training in behavior. The art of letter-writing, it is said, was immensely cultivated. Letters were always flying, not only from house to house, but from room to room. It was a perpetual picnic, a French Revolution in small, an Age of Reason in a patty-pan."

If we except Hawthorne, no member seems to have entertained any dislike for any other member. Hawthorne had a natural aversion for Margaret Fuller, and his savage thrust at her memory is not altogether surprising to those who knew him best. Emerson wrote in his *Historic Notes of Life and Letters in New England*:

"Hawthorne drew some sketches, not happily, as I think; I should rather say, quite unworthy of his genius. No friend who knew Margaret Fuller could recognize her rich and brilliant genius under the dismal mask which the public fancied was meant for her in that disagreeable story."

It is fair to remind the reader that Mr. Frothingham does not think the *Blithedale Romance* was intended as an account of the Brookfarm Association, but it matters little whether it was or was not, since we now have Hawthorne's verdict in his own words, that Margaret was a "humbug."

What came of the Brookfarm experiment? Nothing. It continued about six years and then collapsed, leaving Mr. Ripley heavily in debt. Mr. Frothingham thinks the introduction of Fourierism destroyed it, but it was doomed in the very nature of things. Dr. Holmes says: "The public edifice called the 'Phalanstery' was destroyed by fire in 1846. The association never recovered from this blow, and soon afterward it was dissolved." No doubt the burning of the "Phalanstery" was a severe loss, but the experiment had practically failed before the building was erected. It was a castle in the air from the beginning. It had no foundation. It grew out of dreams, and dissolved, as Frothingham said, "in a song." There are many good things about communistic life, but whatever life be adopted there must be some solid foundation — some scientific basis. There was nothing scientific about Brookfarm; it was only a grand rally of idealists around the most dreamy of dreams. Emerson saw its fate from the first, and that Ripley and his friends were not equally wise is astonishing. The history and fate of Brookfarm show us how the most cultivated minds may be wasted upon empty air, when once the scientific and severely rational method of viewing life and its perplexing problems has been abandoned. Not that poetry and romance are to be cast aside, but that a just appreciation of actual facts must pave the way for wise action.

Millerism made its appearance at the time
the New England idealists were at their
Brookfarm experiment. William Miller, the
founder of the ism that bears his name, served
in the War 1812 and had the rank of captain.
He was a man of ordinary education and of no
theological training. Suddenly the idea pos-
sessed him that he had discovered at what time
the world was to end. He was a fanatic upon
the subject of Bible chronology, and had come
to regard himself as an authority in all the
mathematical problems of Scripture. Careful
students in the pulpit and out of it endeavored
to show him the absurdity of his claim, but all
argument was useless. It was in vain to remind him that the same mistake had been made
in the tenth century, when the famous "God's
Truce" was formed, and that at that time men
were so confident that the consummation of all
things was at hand that many charters opened
with the words, "As the world is now drawing
to its close."

The Apostle Peter, in his second epistle,
predicted the coming of a time when "the
heavens shall pass away with a great noise, and
the elements shall melt with fervent heat; the
earth also and the works that are therein shall
be burnt up." These startling words have
turned the simple wits of many foolish men in

all ages of the Christian era, and in every land where our faith has prevailed. The Saviour said that the final day and hour were to remain a profound secret, unknown to even the angels in heaven, but Miller and ecclesiastical adventurers of his sort are of another opinion, and hesitate not to "rush in where angels fear to tread."

Miller fixed the date of the "final catastrophe" in 1843. It is said that he gathered more than fifty thousand converts. Some of these lost their reason, and more of them were deluded into parting from their property. A number of thrifty farmers who had accumulated small fortunes gave them away. Some bestowed their farms upon unbelievers, and scattered their money in every direction in full faith that the world was about to end. Some were crazy enough to prepare "ascension robes," and upon a certain evening in October, 1843, when it was believed the coming of the Saviour was at hand, hundreds of these deluded Adventists went up to the roofs of their houses clothed in white to meet the Master. Miller never carried his faith so far. He took good care of his property. One who knew him well says that in 1843, as in other years,

" his fields were all clean mown and reaped, and his barns were bursting with their produce. The wood-house was full of wood sawed and piled for winter's use; forty rods of new stone wall had been built that autumn, and the stoneboat or dray stood there with a cargo of boulders ready to be laid on the next day if it should come.''

Miller was asked in 1843 for a subscription toward the building of a small church in an adjoining town, and the petitioner urged a generous donation on the ground that Miller would not want his money long as the world was so near its end. All that the latter-day prophet would give was five dollars' worth of lime. He said: "I believe the Saviour will come to this earth in 1843, but it is possible, though quite unlikely, that I am mistaken. If I am mistaken I shall do well to preserve my property, and if I am right my property can be of no value to any one else. When the Lord comes let Him find me at the post of duty, and in charge of whatever worldly goods it has pleased Him to bestow upon me." On the night when the Saviour was expected Miller put on no angelic vestments, neither did he seek the house-top: on the contrary, he dressed himself in an evening gown, satin vest, and velvet slippers, and he did not forget to fill his pipe with the best tobacco. He added the rôle of philosopher to that of prophet, and though

he believed the end of the world was at hand,
he was careful to bear in mind the ancient
saying, *Humanum est errare.* He resolved to
hold on to his property until the Judge of all
the earth had actually made His appearance,
and to the extent of that resolve he was a wise
man. It was unfortunate for his followers
that their faith was so greatly in excess of
worldly prudence. They paid dearly for a very
unsubstantial air-castle.

Miller's calm and matter-of-fact spirit upon
the evening when he and others expected the
second coming of the Saviour reminds us of
Bishop Burnet's story about Sir Matthew Hale.
A terrific storm occurred in 1666, at a period
when the end of the world was expected. Sir
Matthew Hale sat on the bench in the trial of
an important case. The lightnings dazzled the
eye and the thunders crashed with appalling
power; the assembly was panic-stricken, and
cried out that the day of judgment had begun.
Many dropped upon their knees, and terror
seized upon all. The judge was quiet and unmoved. He calmly ordered that the business
of the court proceed. "But," exclaimed an
excited barrister, "the end of the world has
come." "I do not care," said the judge; "if
the end of all things is at hand, of which there
is no evidence, I desire to be found by my

Maker diligently attending to my daily business." The same story is told of Judge Davenport, of New Haven.

Another remarkable builder of air-castles is Stephen Pearl Andrews, who claims to have discovered a new science which he calls "Universology," and which he says includes all other sciences that have been developed or that ever will be developed in the centuries to come. I was present when, in the city of New York, in 1870, Mr. Andrews explained to a number of literary men, among whom were President Barnard, of Columbia College; Professor E. L. Youmans, Rev. O. B. Frothingham, and Parke Godwin, the foundation principles of his new science. The paper those gentlemen signed upon that occasion may be found in the preface to a book written by Mr. Andrews, and called *The Primary Synopsis of Universology and Alwato*. The book is a curiosity, and I venture to say no one but the author ever read more than five of its two hundred and twenty-four pages, for it is drier and more innutritious than summer dust. Mr. Andrews is still living, and, though well on in years, clings to his "Universology" as Symmes adhered to his "Arctic Hole." His Alwato (pronounced Ahl-wa-to) is a new language, not invented but discovered; it is set forth as the one and only language planted in the universal necessity of things. No other language is competent to express the new science of sciences. I shall always retain many striking remembrances of the wonderful mental power and captivating eloquence of the "Pantarch" (by that name Mr. Andrews calls himself), but I shall ever regret the utter perversion of all that power and eloquence. Had Andrews used his remarkable gifts upon something better than a mere philosophical air-castle he might have secured a conspicuous place among the most brilliant men of the age. Mr. Andrews has published, in addition to the work already named, a very large book called *The Basic Outline of Universology*, and he is also author of *The Science of Society; Discoveries in Chinese; Comparison of the Common Law with the Roman, French, and Spanish Civil Law on Entails and Other Limited Property in Real Estate; Phonographic Reader; Phonographic Reporter; Love, Marriage, and Divorce; French without a Master; The Labor Dollar; Idealogical Etymology;* and various articles in the London *Times* and American papers.

ADDENDUM

Since the foregoing was written, Stephen Pearl Andrews has closed his earthly career,

and we now have before us his completed
work. His death occurred at the home of his
son in the city of New York, on the 21st day
of May, 1886, when he was in the seventy-fifth
year of his age. The funeral, which was held
the following Sunday afternoon in Masonic
Hall on Fifteenth Street, was conducted by
Mr. T. B. Wakeman on behalf of the Manhat-
tan Liberal club, of which the dead philosopher
was long a prominent member.

Mr. Andrews was a remarkable man and de-
serves more than a passing notice. He had
great abilities which, had they been wisely directed, might have given the world a valuable
discoverer in the region of thought, and to
their possessor a worthy and lasting reputation.
He was a daring, original, and brilliant thinker,
an attractive and forcible writer, and an eloquent speaker, being accounted, in the early
part of his life, an orator second only to Wendell Phillips. He is said to have had some understanding of more than twenty languages;
and at one time he was the recipient of many
and distinguished attentions because of his ex-
tensive acquaintance with Oriental literature
and metaphysics. He was a graduate of Am-
herst College, and commenced life with great
promise as a lawyer in New Orleans, where he
had for professional rivals Benjamin Slidell and

others who afterward figured in the Confederacy. He was from the first an avowed Abolitionist; and not in Alabama alone but in Texas, which was at that time an independent republic, he openly assailed the "peculiar institution." In Texas his legal ability was at once discovered, and his services soon came into great demand; but, with the firmness of conviction which followed him from cradle to grave, he refused to become the citizen of a country founded upon human bondage, and declined to engage in any suit involving the question of slavery. His position as an Abolitionist gave serious offence to the people, and in 1843 he narrowly escaped violence at the hands of a mob. He visited England where he sought money and influence with which to destroy the slave power in Texas, and it was the encouragement he received from the British Government that led to the annexation of Texas by the United States. On his return from England, Mr. Andrews went into business in Boston, where he was interested in a new system of shorthand. He was a fine stenographer.

In early life his sympathies were with the evangelical or orthodox interpretation of the Christian faith, but later he became interested in Spiritualism and abandoned the fellowship and teachings of the Church for the vagaries of

Owen, Davis, and Edmonds. His change of belief was undoubtedly the result of sincere conviction. It separated him not only from early associations (his father, Elisha Andrews, was a prominent Baptist clergyman), but from a multitude of influential friends, and closed against him the open door of popular recognition and applause. From Spiritualism he naturally advanced to what has been mildly called "a broad doctrine of social freedom"—a doctrine that gave great offence, and that brought his name into an ill-repute from which it never recovered. His crowning, and certainly his most original work, was comprehended in the three words, "Universology," "Integralism," and "Alwato." These covered the science of all sciences, the philosophy of all philosophies, and the one only true language planted by nature in the very heart of the universe. That he had discovered such science, philosophy, and language he fully believed, and upon them as upon a sure foundation, he proceeded to construct a social organization to be called "The Pantarchy," of which he was to be "Pantarch," or directing and inspiring centre of all. For many years Mr. Andrews toiled in neglect and sometimes in poverty (he was once wealthy) to perfect and introduce his great discovery; and now, after a life generously, I had

s

almost said nobly, wasted in building a castle
in the air, he has descended into that remorse-
less silence which surely awaits every dreamer
who ministers not to the solid and substantial
welfare of mankind, but with sad and mistaken
enthusiasm pursues and cherishes a phantom.
The grave of Charles Fourier in the Cimetière
de Montmartre and that of Stephen Pearl Andrews in Woodlawn are melancholy witnesses
to the folly of wasting time and talent in
the wild though fascinating pursuit of the
impossible.

HAFIZ

ABOUT two miles to the northeast of Shiraz is the tomb of Hafiz Mohammed Shems-ed-Deen (one who knows the Koran and traditions: Sun of Religion), also called Lishan-al-Ghaid (Voice of Mystery), but commonly known as Hafiz. The precise date of the distinguished poet's birth is not known, but falls somewhere in the early part of the fourteenth century; the date on his tombstone is 791 H. (1388 A.D.). His youth was marked by great dislike for every kind of restraint. He was joyous, free, and light-hearted; a bold innovator, and a merry companion. A host of friends gathered around him and sunned themselves in his genial wit. When a boy his eloquence attracted attention, and the tropical beauty of his early poems won for him the appellation Tschegerleb or Sugarlip. Some say Zikhr, the Mohammedan Elijah, brought him a draught from the fountain of living water, but we think it more likely that his genius was nursed upon red wine from the warm breasts of the grape. His remarkable precocity and great promise secured him a place as teacher in the royal family of the house of Muzaffer, and a new college was established for the accommodation of his pupils who came from every direction to sit at the feet of a philosopher who added to the wisdom of a religious teacher and the skill of a grammarian, the seductive arts of a lover and the persuasive eloquence of a poet. Hafiz, like Abelard, joined in himself seemingly opposite characteristics. The gifted and illustrious founder of the Paraclete was not only a profound theologian and dialectician, but a popular poet and an ardent lover. Both were famous teachers and drew to their lectures students from every part of the then civilized world. Both were disliked and persecuted by the conservative religious classes. So great was the orthodox religious clamor against Hafiz that the priests refused to read the Persian liturgy at his funeral; their prejudices were overcome, however, and the poet was accorded a magnificent burial.

Hafiz was the poet of love, wine, flowers, and beauty. His entire life was an illustration of a famous motto over a sun-dial: *Horas non numero nisi serenas.* He counted none but the cloudless hours. He was, what Emerson calls him, "the prince of Persian poets"—Pindar,

Anacreon, Horace, and Burns in one. He hated
hypocrisy and cant in both love and religion,
and so independent was his spirit that he refused every honor and passed his entire life in
the humble condition of a dervish. No arbitrary restriction could have any force with
him. Mind and heart were free as the wind,
and life must follow after them. Thus he
put aside all mediators, "Take example of
the roses, that live direct on dew and sunshine.
They never question after Moses; and why
should you?" He said of religion, "The objects of all faiths are alike. All men seek their
beloved; and all the world is love's dwelling."
He had no need for church or mosque. Neither
Bible nor Koran troubled his conscience. To
wash out from the priest all superstition and
every remnant of ecclesiastical acerbity, he pro-
posed to "draw the cowl through a brook of
wine." Some read in his songs deep spiritual
meanings, and think to find a divine sense un-
under the most amorous and bacchanalian lines.
We take the poet where we find him and at his
own word. He says, "I hide me in my song."
He is what he sings—that and nothing more.
Walt Whitman is the only poet we know of
who resembles Hafiz in this absolute identifi-
cation of himself with his verse. Whitman
writes:

"I celebrate myself, and sing myself,
And what I assume you shall assume,
For every atom belonging to me as good be-
longs to you."

Hafiz sings:

"Oft have I said, I say it once more,
I, a wanderer, do not stray from myself.
I am a kind of parrot; the mirror is holden to me;
What the Eternal says, I, stammering, say again.
Give me what you like; I eat thistles as roses,
And according to my food I grow and give.
Scorn me not, but know I have the pearl,
And am only seeking one to receive it." [1]

He gives this account of himself:

"Dervish! does your galling envy make it hurt
    you?
When you think that Hafiz' sins the prize of virtue
Win? But he that sins like him, O formal weeper!
In God's mercy-ocean only sinks the deeper.

"My drunkenness is not a fault of mine;
For drunken came I from the hand Divine,
Which kneaded up my nascent clay with wine.
Therefore, when, dry and hard, I fainting pine,
No moisture suits me like the yeasty vine."

[1] The translations in this paper are mostly from Emerson's
Essay on "Persian Poetry."

His religion is a perpetual falling in love with the beautiful daughters of Allah, and all the wealth of his faith is poured out with that of his heart in celebrating the lovely qualities of his mistress. Nothing in any sacrament or mystery is too sacred for this worship. Bible, Koran, and whatever he can find is pressed into the service. In this idealized, but none the less material love, he finds a balm for every hurt and a solace for every woe:

" The world is bitter as the juice from aloes beaten;
  Yet know I lips which all its bitterness can
    sweeten."

He boldly follows love without forecast and trusts himself to the exigency of the moment. If love conduct into mazes of bewilderment and labyrinths of perplexity it will be all the same to him. Courage and submission, the two fatalistic virtues, hold as good in love as in religion. He asks no metaphysical questions, neither will he puzzle his mind about their solution. He lives for the present hour and leaves eternity to the priests. He is at home in the world of nature and delights to live with birds, flowers, and all simple-hearted and joyous creatures. His soul is aglow with the morning red, and his songs are full of wine and music.

His divan celebrates every phase of passion.
Its lines, like a rushing wind, lift us from the
earth, and hurry us on from one object of delight to another, and whether it be Leila's
locks, Zuleika's cheek, or the fascinating eyes
of the heavenly Houris it matters little, for
what Hafiz shows us must be beautiful. Even
common and prosaic loves are changed by him
into the most glowing romance of Oriental passion. He tells us:

> " The chemist of love
> Will this perishing mould,
> Were it made out of mire,
> Transmute into gold."

In two exquisite stanzas he shows the world
how recklessly his heart abandons itself to love:

> " I know this perilous love-lane
> No whither the traveller leads,
> Yet my fancy the sweet scent of
> Thy tangled tresses feeds.

> " In the midnight of thy locks,
> I renounce the day;
> In the ring of thy rose-lips,
> My heart forgets to pray."

But he who mistakes Hafiz for a mere sensualist is far from understanding either man or

poet. His verses are as they appear, and are not oracles; yet they are vast treasure-houses filled with the riches of the mind and the more costly treasures of the heart. If his songs and philosophy undermined the foundations of the established faith of his age and country, it is clear to us, and was to many of his own time, that the destruction was in the interest of truth. He exalted health, gladness, nature, and humanity, over superstition, disease, and brooding melancholy. Neither the *welt-schmerz* nor the *selbst-schmerz* of the Germans had any part in his life. He was a child of the sun, and all his songs were sunbeams. He seized upon the common experiences of mankind and upon the most trivial objects, and glorified them with new spirit and recreative genius. Even the wildest drinking songs and most amorous verses have this redeeming feature. The world is richer and better for nearly every line it has received from the lovely and health-bestowing soul of Hafiz:

" Sweet Hafiz is not dead, although his body turned
    To dust in Eastern Shiraz centuries ago.
He lives and strikes the lyre which in his hand
    then burned:
This day his thoughts through Western na-
    tions sound and glow."

THE TOMB OF ABELARD AND HELOISE

THE sacred soil of Père-la-Chaise holds the precious dust of the most gifted sons and daughters of beautiful France. Poets, musicians, artists, ecclesiastics, men of science, and heroes of peace and war all slumber together on the banks of the Seine and under the blue sky of the land they loved and served so well. In that picturesque cemetery rest the earthly tenements of Visconti, the architect of the new Louvre; Poinsot, the great mathematician; Alfred de Musset, the poet of society; Laromiguière, the distinguished professor of philosophy; the illustrious Arago; the statesman and prime minister of 1832, Casimir Périer; the immortal Rossini; Mlle. Rachel, the actress; Marshal Kellermann; Countess Demidoff; General Gouviou St. Cyr; Scribe, the dramatic author; Viscomte de Martignac; Marshal Suchet; Madame Cottin, the novelist; Beaumarchais, the dramatist; Baron Larrey, the surgeon of Napoleon I.; Marshal Ney; General Foy; the poet Béranger; Geoffroy-Saint-Hilaire; Pradier; the great astronomer Laplace; Molière; the Marquis de Clermont-Gallerande, who placed himself between Louis XVI. and the mob, on the never-to-be-forgotten 10th of August; Volney; Theron de Morny; the Queen and elder Prince of Oude; Honoré de Balzac; Talma; Bellini; Rubini; and the famous Adèle Terchout. There they all repose under green grass and snowy marble—friend and foe, saint and sinner, the lover and his mistress, the solitary genius who stood apart from the world and the iris-hued butterfly of changing fashion. But from this vast wilderness of graves, covered with historic and romantic associations and garlanded with wreaths, the pilgrim of sentiment turns aside to view first of all the *chapelle sepulcrale d'Héloïse et d'Abélard.* The tomb of the "saint of passion" and her famous but unfortunate lover is covered with floral tributes from all parts of the world. Thither journey old and young with fond remembrance of youthful ardor or with the glowing experience of its delightful flame.

> " Come to yon stately dome,
> With arch and turret, every shapely stone
> Breathing the legends of the Paraclete;
> Where slumber Abelard and Heloise,

'Neath such a world of wreaths, that scarce ye see
Their marble forms recumbent, side by side."

Peter Abelard died in 1142, and Heloise in
1163.[1] They were at first buried in the same

[1] Abelard's last letter to Heloise before his departure from
the scene of his earthly cares affords a touching illustration of
his constancy :

"You have been the victim of my love, become now the
victim of my repentance. Accomplish faithfully that which
God demands of you. It is a manifestation of His greatness
that the only foundation of His goodness to man lies in our
weaknesses ; let us mourn over ours at the foot of the altar.
He only waits for our contrition and humility to put an end
to our misfortunes. Let our repentance be as public as our
crimes were. We are a sad example of the imprudence of
youth. Let us show our generation and posterity that the
repentance of our errors has merited their forgiveness ; and
let us make them admire in us the power of the grace which
has been able to triumph over the tyranny of our passions.
Do not be discouraged by occasional returns of tenderness,
for it is a virtue to combat and overcome such attacks. May
your knowledge of human weaknesses teach you to support
the faults of your companions. If I have corrupted your
mind, compromised your salvation, tarnished your reputation,
destroyed your honor, pardon me, and remember that it is
Christian mercy to forgive the evil I have done you. Providence calls us to Him ; do not oppose Him, Heloise. Do
not write to me any more. This is the last letter you will
receive from me, but in whatsoever place I die I shall leave
directions for my body to be conveyed to Paraclete. Then I
shall require prayers and not tears ; then only you will see me
to fortify your piety, and my corpse, more eloquent than myself, will teach you what one loves when one loves a man."

Before his death an interview was brought about between

crypt in the Paraclete, and there reposed side
by side until 1497, when their communion in
death was pronounced a scandal to the Church,
and priestly hands assigned them different

him and St. Bernard, through the intermediary of Peter the
Venerable. Such an interview was in itself an historical episode, and one well worthy of depiction by the poet or painter.

When death came to him on the 21st of April, 1142, in his
sixty-third year, he was prepared to meet it, and one of the
most remarkable men of his age passed from this life, let us
hope, to another and happier world, where the wicked cease
from troubling, and the weary are at rest.

In accordance with his last wishes his body was entombed
at Paraclete, the chief mourner being his wife Heloise. For
twenty-two years she lived to watch by his tomb, the most
constant of women, the most unfortunate of wives. On the
17th of May, 1164, the final act in this touching drama was
performed according to the wishes of the unhappy couple, and
the body of Heloise was lowered into the tomb of Abelard.
A popular legend asserts that on opening the tomb for the
interment of Heloise, the faithful husband who had so long
awaited the coming of his beloved wife, extended his fleshless
arms to receive her.

The united remains of husband and wife were not permitted to rest tranquilly in the grave where they had been
deposited. The vicissitudes of their lives seemed to be
continued after their death. In the year 1800 their bones
were transported to the cemetery of Père-la-Chaise, Paris,
where a handsome Gothic monument was erected over them.
The visitor to the cemetery will find the tomb in the older
part of the grounds on the right of the main entrance, and
will perceive by the *immortelles*, in all stages of freshness and
decay, heaped upon it, that there are still sympathetic souls
who mourn the fate of those unhappy lovers of the Middle
Age.—*The Westminster Review.*

tombs. Well would it be for the Church of
Rome had no greater scandal ever stained her
scarlet robe. Two centuries later the lovers
were changed to a new crypt and restored to
each other. In 1766 Marie de la Rochefou-
cauld erected a monument to their memory,
and a little later Madame de Roney de la Ro-
chefoucauld, niece of the former, and last abbess of Paraclete, inscribed over their common
tomb the following epitaph:

Hic,
Sub eodem marmore, jacent,
Hujus, Monasterii
Conditor, Petrus Abælardus,
Et Abbatissa Prima, Heloisa,
Olim studiis, ingenio, amore, infaustis nuptiis,
Et pœnitentia,
Nunc æterno, quod speramus, felicitate,
Conjuncti,
Petrus obiit XX. Prima Aprilis, MCXLII.,
Heloisa, XVII. Maii, MCLXIII.

In 1792 all French convents were destroyed,
and among them the Paraclete. The bones of
the lovers were again taken from their resting
place and were borne in solemn state and with
great pomp to a church, where an elaborate
funeral was accorded them. It must have been
a strange scene, priests reading prayers, choirs

singing hymns, and the people mourning and weeping for the dead of more than six centuries ago. And yet was not the sorrow perfectly natural? "All the world loves a lover," and these tributes were not to Abelard and Heloise only but to human love in every age and land. After a funeral discourse, the coffin, in which the gifted founder and the passionate abbess of Paraclete were separated from each other by a thin partition of lead, was placed in a vault under the Chapel of St. Leger. There they remained eight years, when Lucien Bonaparte had them removed to the Jardin du Musée Français and deposited in a magnificent sepulchral chapel builded out of choice stones taken from the ruins of Paraclete and of the abbey of St. Denis. Two more changes brought them to Père-la-Chaise, where, on the 6th of November, 1817, they were laid to rest.

We have no authentic picture of either Abelard or Heloise, but Lenoir (see the *Notice Historique*, etc., par M. Alex. Lenoir, imprimée à Paris en 1815, p. 4, *et seq.*), speaking of the devoted abbess of Paraclete, says:

" The inspection of the bones of her body, which we have examined with care, has convinced us that she was, like Abelard, of large stature, and finely proportioned. The head of Heloise is finely proportioned; the forehead, smoothly formed, well rounded and in harmony with the other parts of the face, still expresses perfect beauty. This head, which was so well organized, has been moulded under my own eyes for the execution of the bust of Heloise, which has been modelled by M. de Seine.''

Abelard's personal appearance may be gathered from contemporaneous literature. Charles de Rémusat wrote in his *Vie d'Abélard* :

"In the midst of this attentive and obedient multitude (Abelard's five thousand pupils) was often seen passing, a man with a large forehead, with a vivid and fiery look, with a noble bearing, whose beauty still preserved the brilliancy of youth, while taking the more marked traits and the deeper hues of full virility. His grave and elegant dress, the severe luxury of his person, the simple elegance of his manners, which were by turns affable and haughty; an attitude imposing, gracious, and not without that indolent negligence which follows confidence in success, and the habitual exercise of power; the respect of those who followed in his train, who were arrogant to all except him; the eager curiosity of the multitude, all, when he went to his lectures or returned to his dwelling, followed by his disciples, still charmed by his speech, all announced a master the most powerful in the schools, the most renowned in the world, the most loved in the city. The crowd in the streets stopped to gaze at him as he passed; the people rushed to the doors of their houses and women gazed at him from their windows. Paris had adopted him as her child, as her ornament and her light. Paris was proud of Abelard, and celebrated the name of which, after seven centuries, the city of all glories and oblivions has preserved the popular memory."

Charles de Rémusat's picture is taken from early and authentic records. Abelard was the greatest scholar and the most gifted thinker and teacher of his age. Of himself he leaves this account in his published works: "My name was then so great, the graces of youth and the perfection of form gave me a superiority so unquestionable, that from whatever woman I might have honored with my love, I should have feared no repulse." Dr. John William Draper, in his *History of the Intellectual Development of Europe*, writes: "The love of Heloise seems in our eyes to be justified by his extraordinary intellectual power." The love may be justified, for it was pure and womanly, but how shall we reconcile it with perfidy and indifference to her good name on his part? Can we forget that while he was expounding Ezekiel to five thousand students of theology, he was also composing amorous songs to Heloise and publishing them for all

Paris to sing? Can we forget his confession
that he became her instructor with the deliber-
ate purpose of initiating her into the mysteries
of love? Heloise was a woman of remarkable
talent and acquirements; so great was her
learning that at the age of seventeen her fame
extended over all France. Her intellectual
power and culture fitted her for the confidence
and companionship of that wonderful man
whose lectures and discussions opened the way
for scholasticism, and actually introduced the
celebrated doctrines of Nominalism and Realism, though the terms themselves were not
coined before the end of the twelfth century.
Her love for him, pure, deep, and self-sacrificing, merited a return as noble and generous.
Alas! for human nature, that the womanly and
glowing heart of Heloise should receive for all
its measureless wealth of passion a love so
earthly and selfish. Only the boundless and
deathless love of Heloise saves Abelard from
being a base and perfidious seducer. She
placed at his feet, a willing offering, everything
that a woman cherishes. For his sake she
faced the indignant Fulbert, accepted mater-
nity without marriage, and chose shame. And
later, after she had reluctantly consented to
marriage, she refused to receive the felicitations
addressed to her, and sacrificed her name as

wife for his fame as a public scholar and
teacher. "I call God to witness," wrote
Heloise, "that if Augustus the emperor of the
world, had deemed me worthy of his hand, and
would give me the universe for a throne, the
name of your concubine would have been more
glorious to me than that of his empress."
When fearful retribution came to Abelard she
rose above passion and remained true to his
nobler manhood.   There must have been something better than we know of in the nature of
a man who could attract and obtain so great a
sacrifice from a priestess so exalted. "Perfect
love casteth out fear."   High order of intellect
requires for its equilibrium a glowing and ardent
nature.   The finer the mental organization of
a man the more he demands sensitive, delicate,
and responsive traits.   Such qualities Clotilde
de Vaux brought to the great mind of the philosopher Comte.   Of her he wrote in his preface and dedication of the first volume of his
Système de Politique positive, "She is associated
with all my thoughts and with all my feelings."
In these touching words he bids farewell to the
idol of his heart—they were written when she
had been dead six years:

"Adieu, my unchangeable companion!   Adieu,
my holy Clotilde!   Thy celestial inspiration will

dominate the remainder of my life, public as well as private, and preside over my progress toward perfection, purifying my sentiments, ennobling my thoughts and elevating my conduct. Perhaps as the principal reward of the grand tasks yet left for me to contemplate and complete under thy powerful invocation, I shall inseparably write thy name with my own in the latest remembrances of a grateful humanity."

Clotilde Chiarini, who won to herself the noble heart of one of the most cultivated and scholarly men of the age and country, and then, when she drew him to her arms, looked coldly into his eyes and read him a homily on morals, sleeps in an unknown grave in some neglected corner of Père-la-Chaise; but the sweet "saint of passion," the Heloise of every tender heart, rests under garlands and floral tributes from all parts of the world. And to her grave journey old and young with fond remembrance of youthful ardor or with the glowing experience of its delightful flame. Sings the poet:

"I see grand tombs of France's lesser dead;
Colossal steeds, white pyramids, still red
At base with blood, still torn with shot and shell,
To testify that here the commune fell;
And yet I turn once more from all of these,
And stand before the tomb of Heloise."

A great love triumphs over death. In the beautiful drama of *Ion*, when the noble Greek is about to surrender his life to the demands of inexorable fate, his Clementhe asks if they shall meet again, and the response expresses the feeling of every heart:

"I have asked that dreadful question of the hills that look eternal—of the clear streams that flow forever—of the stars among whose fields of azure my raised spirit has walked in glory. All are dumb. But as I gaze upon thy living face, I feel that there is something in love that mantles through its beauty, and cannot wholly perish. We shall meet again, Clementhe."

The author of *Canticles* tells us that "love is stronger than death." "I saw her but once, and shall love her forever," has been the experience of not a few of our race.

It was an ancient Jewish custom of marriage for the wedded pair to drink from the same crystal cup and then break it in pieces. This symbolized the frailty of earthly possessions and the transitoriness of earthly felicity. But if the education remains after the cup has been dashed upon the earth, it may be after all, as the Laureate sings:

> " Better to have loved and lost
> Than never to have loved at all."

THE SORROWFUL STORY OF PAOLO
AND FRANCESCA

TOUCHING and sad as is the story of
Abelard and Heloise, even greater sorrow
and more bewitching romance gather around
the love and fate of Paolo, the handsome, and
Francesca da Rimini. All who have found delight in the page of Dante and in Petrarch's
Triumph of Love will approach the grave of the
lovers with the feeling that they are treading
upon sacred ground. Francesca was the beautiful daughter of Guido Vecchio da Polenta,
Lord of Ravenna. Her father gave her in marriage to Gianciotto, the son of Malatesta, Lord
of Rimini, an ugly, offensive, and deformed
dwarf. Paolo, her brother-in-law, won her heart
and drew her away from the path of virtue.
Gianciotto, finding them together, slew them
both and cast them into a common grave.
Dante, Petrarch, Boccaccio, Leigh Hunt, Silvio
Pellico, and Ary Scheffer have surrounded the
tale with literary and artistic attractions, and
yet the reader naturally inquires how it differs

86

from any other romance of seduction and
adultery. The morality of the beautiful Francesca's conduct rests on the fact that she was
deceived into marriage with a man who was
represented to be the opposite of what he really
was. Gianciotto was a man of great ambition,
and aspired to a position of unusual wealth and
distinction, but he was, as has been said, a
deformed and ugly dwarf. Francesca's father,
moved by mercenary motives, desired to have
him for a son-in-law, and, knowing that his
proud and cultivated daughter would refuse his
request were she to see what manner of man
had been selected for her, he entered into a
conspiracy with Gianciotto to secure Francesca
for his bride by deputy. Gianciotto accordingly
commissioned his brother Paolo, who was exceedingly handsome and courteous, to pass himself off for the intended husband. He courted
the proud and lovely daughter of Guido Vecchio da Polenta and easily won her heart.
The marriage ceremony was a cruel and shameful deception. She pledged her hand to Paolo,
and in the evening was conveyed to the bridal
chamber of Gianciotto, whom she had never
seen. She did not discover the deceit till the
morning ensuing the marriage. When she
beheld the dwarf rise from her side she hated
and despised him. He had deeply wronged

her, and she was bound to him by no obligation of either morality or religion. Of course
all this does not justify the conduct of Paolo.
He was party to the deception. He won her
love by fraud and lost his heart in the dangerous game. It so happened that Paolo and
Francesca lived in the same house, and Gianciotto being absent on business, love united
them without sanction of law. When Gianciotto returned he discovered them together.
Let Boccaccio tell the story:

" Arriving, he went straight to the door, and
finding it locked inside, called to his lady to come
out; Paolo thinking to escape suddenly through an
opening in the wall, by means of which there was
descent into another room, and so to conceal his
fault, threw himself into the opening, telling the
lady to go and open the door. But this did
not turn out as he expected; for the hem of a
mantle which he had on caught upon a nail, and
the lady opening the door meantime, in the belief
that all would be well by reason of Paolo's not being there, Gianciotto caught sight of Paolo as he
was detained by the hem of the mantle and straight-
way ran with his dagger in his hand to kill him;
whereupon the lady to prevent it ran between them;
but Gianciotto having lifted the dagger, and put the
whole force of his arm into the blow, there came
to pass what he had not desired—namely, that he

struck the dagger into the bosom of the lady before he could reach Paolo; by which accident, being as one who had loved the lady better than himself, he withdrew the dagger and again struck at Paolo and slew him; and so leaving them both dead he hastily went his way and betook him to his wonted affairs; and the next morning the two lovers with many tears were buried together in the same grave.''

Dante met the lovers in hell, and there learned from their own lips the story of their love and ruin. Longfellow thus literally translates the scene:

> " Then unto them I turned me, and I spake,
> And I began:—' Thine agonies, Francesca,
> Sad and compassionate to weeping make me.
> But tell me, at the time of those sweet sighs,
> By what and in what manner Love conceded
> That you should know your dubious desires ? '
> And she to me:—' There is no greater sorrow
> Than to be mindful of the happy time
> In misery, and that thy Teacher knows.
> But, if to recognize the earliest root
> Of love in us thou hast so great desire,
> I will do even as he who weeps and speaks.
> One day we reading were for our delight
> Of Launcelot, how Love did him enthrall.
> Alone we were and without fear.
> Full many a time our eyes together drew
> That reading, and drove the color from our faces;

But one point was it that o'ercame us.
When as we read of the much longed-for smile
Being by such a noble lover kissed,
This one, who ne'er from me shall be divided,
Kissed me upon the mouth all palpitating.
Galeotto was the book and he who wrote it.
That day no farther did we read therein.'
And all the while one spirit uttered this,
The other one did weep so, that, for pity,
I swooned away as if I had been dying,
And fell, even as a dead body falls." [1]

Boccaccio differs from Dante in assuming that the lovers were guiltless of the crime for which Gianciotto slew them. And while Dante sends them to the abode of misery, the charitable Boccaccio sends them to heaven, much to the satisfaction of all tender hearts and sympathetic readers. The story is involved in some doubts, and Leigh Hunt, anxious to state only the truth, gives us, in the appendix to his *Italian Poets*, what he calls

"*The only Particulars hitherto really Ascertained respecting the History of Paolo and Francesca.*

[1] The story told by Dante in matchless verse, and represented by Flaxman upon canvas that once seen can never be forgotten, is somewhat changed, to heighten dramatic effect, by a clever writer of plays, Mr. George H. Baker, in his *Francesca da Rimini*. The original account of the tragedy has been republished by Charles Griarte in his *Malatestas of Rimini*.

"1. Francesca was daughter of Guido Vecchio da Polenta, Lord of Ravenna.

"2. She was married to Gianciotto, surnamed the Lame, one of the sons of Malatesta da Verrucchio, Lord of Rimini.

"3. Gianciotto the Lame had a brother named Paolo the Handsome, who was a widower and left a son.

"4. Twelve years after Francesca's marriage, by which time she had become mother of a son and of a daughter who survived her, she and her brother-in-law Paolo were slain together by the husband and buried in one grave.

"5. Two hundred years afterward the grave was opened and the bodies found lying together in silken garments, the silk itself being entire."

Hunt may be right or wrong. The affair may have occurred twelve years after the marriage, but is far more likely to have followed immediately upon her discovery of the deception practised upon her by Gianciotto. We shall content ourselves with tradition and believe in the early romance until further facts are discovered.

The skeletons of the lovers were found in the tomb where they had rested together, each in the other's embrace, for two centuries. All the bones were in perfect order, not one was missing. The garments remained, though the

soft parts of their bodies had crumbled away;
and the silken mantle which enfolded them,
and which had been supplied by the citizens,
who viewed their punishment as too severe for
the offence, was in good condition.

THE SONNET

THE critic may discuss poetic license, but the poet knows that the limitations of verse are quite as pronounced and ubiquitous. The "thus far and no farther" of prosody faces the bard on every side, and like the ghost in the play will not down. There is that prison of Guittone d'Arezzo, the sonnet—a composition strictly fourteen lines deep by ten syllables wide and confined to a single idea. Professor Bain must have had it in mind when he wrote:

"The absence of restraints, of severe conditions in fine art, allows a flush and ebullience, an opulence of production, that is often called the highest genius. The Shakesperian profusion of images would have been reduced to one half, if not less, by the self-imposed restraints of Pope, Gray, or Tennyson."

Whatever restricts or prevents the free play of genius is a literary obstruction and should be removed. For what are the rules of prosody and all the arts and refinements of verse if not to develop the soul of poetry? Laws are necessary, but they must be so ample and elastic that no one pursuing art with skill and reverence shall feel restraint. The architect had a plan for the Parthenon and the sculptor did not chip at random when he made the Venus de Milo, but architect and sculptor were free as are the winds of heaven. Genius breaks through every restraint and becomes a law unto herself. Walt Whitman shows us in his *Leaves of Grass* how independent it is possible for genius to become. That poets feel the restraint is clear from their own confessions. Early Italian poets borrowed from the troubadours the *terza rima*, and made good use of its triple music; but after a time the *terza rima* bound them hand and foot. Then there was a great clanking of chains and crying out against tyranny, and bards of every name and description demanded deliverance from the prisons they had so laboriously constructed. Let Matthew Arnold describe the severe conditions of poetry in a graceful sonnet:

" That son of Italy who tried to blow,
    Ere Dante came, the trump of sacred song,
    In his light youth, amid a festal throng,
Sat with his bride to see a public show.

" Fair was the bride, and on her front did glow
    Youth like a star; and what to youth belong—
    Gay raiment, sparkling gauds, elation strong.
A prop gave way! crash fell a platform! lo,

"'' Mid struggling sufferers, hurt to death, she lay!
     Shuddering, they drew her garments off — and
       found
     A robe of sackcloth next the smooth white skin.

" Such, poets, is your bride, the Muse! young, gay,
     Radiant, adorn'd outside; a hidden ground
     Of thought and of austerity within.''

"That son of Italy" was Giacopone di Todi, and his sad discovery illustrates the hidden bondage of a poetry held in the inelastic fetters of literary restraint. Yet Petrarch, the most distinguished of Italian sonneteers, completed the prison founded by Guittone d'Arezzo, and gave the sonnet but two rhymes in its first eight lines. Few Englishmen could be at home in such narrow quarters, and so the Earl of Surrey deliberately abandoned the archetypal form of the sonnet, and wrote with three quatrains, each with two rhymes of its own, and a couplet at the end to make the requisite fourteen lines. Spenser followed with other innovations and wrote sonnets in blank verse, finally adopting three quatrains with one common rhyme. James Ashcroft Noble, in an article on "The Sonnet in England," in the *Contemporary Review* for September, 1880, writes:

" To a true student of sonnet-development the notion that a sonnet might be advantageously writ-

ten in four ordinary elegiac quatrains and a couplet,
or in seven couplets, or with any other arrangements
of the rhymes than the two or three which had become established by repeated experiments, would
not sound one whit more absurd than the theory
that a sonnet might be written in thirteen, or in
fifteen, or in any other number of lines; for if, in a
purely arbitrary form, the canons of composition
sanctioned by an established nomenclature may be
violated in one particular, they may be violated in
all, and when this violation is accomplished, where
is the sonnet?"

It is possible to make English sonnets after
the Italian pattern. Lady Dacre and others
have shown in their translations from Petrarch,
Michael Angelo, and Vittoria Colonna how
much is possible to persistent and cultivated
genius, even when confined by the restraints
of Guittone d'Arezzo and his followers. But
are the restraints justified by results? What is
accomplished through them that could not be
accomplished without them? In the language
of Lord Macaulay: "What is the particular
virtue which belongs to fourteen as distinguished from all other numbers? Does it arise
from its being a multiple of seven?" Are
there not decided objections to a rigid rule of
fourteen? The very soul of poetry is imagination, but will imagination sing more sweetly

for having its wings clipped? An insurmount-
able objection to the sonnet arises from the fact
that you can have no more water in your cup
than the cup will hold. The narrow compass
and rigid laws of the sonnet cramp and fetter
the indwelling spirit. Hence the sonnet is
given over to the expression of love and
personal experience. The best thing said of
the sonnet is by Lorenzo de' Medici : "The
necessary brevity of the sonnet makes it essential that not one redundant word should
be made use of; the genuine subject-matter of
the sonnet should be some distinct, fine idea,
embodied in corresponding language and in
few verses, avoiding all harshness and obscurity." So we are to understand that the peculiar merit of the sonnet is its narrow compass
—its restrictions prevent redundancy.

A delicate sonnet from the pen of an American lady, Mary B. Dodge, and called *The
Sonnet-Maker*, displays at once the slavery and
final reconciliation to literary bondage to which
the sonnet is self-subjected:

" No couch of roses (yielding sweets exprest
  Of endless summer) with blue canopy,
  Wrought of the whole wide heaven's immensity,
And starred with stars from boundless east to west,
Is that on which the sonneteer may rest!

If, in like space, his fancy's dreams were free
   To breathe unstrained the breath of poesie,
Soft were his stages to life's laureled crest.

" But mark what liberty doth him await
   In whom the sonnet's rule has preference bred,
To find repose in so constrained estate:
   Parnassian meads his muse's feet may tread
And he be borne by them by beauty's gate
   Yet bound a prisoner on Procrustean bed! "

The "robe of sackcloth next the smooth white skin" and the "Procrustean bed" may become, through long use, as delightful to the sonnet-maker as was the bed of potsherds to Mary Alacoque. Wordsworth was so entirely at home in the sonnet that its bondage was pastime. He describes his experience in a *Sonnet on the Sonnet:*

" Nuns fret not at their convent's narrow room;
And hermits are contented with their cells;
And students with their pensive citadels;
Maids at the wheel, the weaver at his loom,
Sit blithe and happy; bees that soar for bloom,
High as the highest peak of Furness-fells,
Will murmur by the hour in foxglove bells:
In truth the prison, unto which we doom
Ourselves, no prison is: and hence to me,
In sundry moods, 't was pastime to be bound
Within the Sonnet's scanty plot of ground;

Pleased if some souls (for such there needs must be)
Who have felt the weight of too much liberty,
Should find brief solace there, as I have found."

The sonnet is peculiarly Italian, yet ever since
its acclimatization under English skies, for
which we may thank Sir Thomas Wyatt, it
has been cultivated by the best poets. We
scarcely need the good advice of Wordsworth,
"Scorn not the sonnet," when we remember
that the fourteen-lined exotic numbers among
its friends Sir Philip Sidney, Spenser, Shakespeare, Milton, Keats, and Elizabeth Barrett
Browning. The true Italian sonnet is a love
poem, and subjects everything to the purposes
of passion—the arts of war and the hopes of
religion are alike made tributary to the ardent
flame. How glowing and yet religious were
the sonnets Petrarch addressed to Laura, who,
if a real person, of which there is some doubt,
was Laura de Noves, the wife of Hugo de
Sade, of Avignon. Concerning a peculiarly
warm sonnet dedicated to her, the poet made
this entry in his diary· "God willing, *Domino
jubente*, I began this sonnet on the tenth of
September, at daybreak, after my morning
prayers." A modern poet would hardly think
it worth while to say his prayers before indit-
ing an amorous sonnet to another man's wife.
Byron's inquiry is not without force.—

" Think you, if Laura had been Petrarch's wife,
    He would have written sonnets all his life ? "

Perhaps Laura was all the more beautiful because beyond his reach.   How beautiful she
appeared to her poet-lover we may learn from
his own pen :

" In what ideal world or part of heaven
    Did nature find the model of that face
    And form, so fraught with loveliness and grace,
    In which, to our creation, she has given
    Her prime proof of creative power above ?
    What fountain nymph or goddess ever let
    Such lovely tresses float, of gold refined,
    Upon the breeze, or, in a single mind,
    Where have so many virtues ever met,
    E'en though those charms have slain my bos-
        om's weal ?
    He knows not love who has not seen her eyes
    Turn when she sweetly speaks, or smiles, or sighs,
    Or how the power of love can hurt or heal. "

That Laura was insensible and of cold heart
there is no reason to believe; but the record of
the poet, contained in his *Dialogues with St.
Augustin*, makes it clear beyond all question
that Laura was pure and upright :

" Untouched by my prayers, unvanquished by
my arguments, unmoved by my flattery, she re-

mained faithful to her sex's honor; she resisted her own young heart, and mine, and a thousand, thousand, thousand things, which must have conquered any other. She remained unshaken. A woman taught me the duty of a man! to persuade me to keep the path of virtue, her conduct was at once an example and a reproach; and when she beheld me break through all bounds and rush blindly to the precipice she had the courage to abandon me rather than follow me."

The English sonnet is unlike its Italian predecessor in the subject of its song; the former delights in philosophy, and often in metaphysics, while the latter concerns itself chiefly with passion. Who can imagine Milton, the "God-gifted organ voice of England," celebrating the personal charms of Leonora Baroni in the spirit of Petrarch or of Dante? When Petrarch appeared in the streets of Avignon men and women were wont to whisper, "there goes the lover of Laura!" The sturdy old Puritan poet had little time and no inclination for fields of merely terrestrial enchantment; his muse ascended to heaven and received inspiration from the celestial choir. Spenser's sonnets are correctly described as clear and cold. Wordsworth's are contemplative, rural, and domestic. Those of Matthew Arnold are ethical and reflective. The sonnets of Shakespeare

may be exceptions to the rule, but they
are so irregular that some excellent critics
refuse to call them sonnets. Lamb says of
Sidney's poetry, "It is stuck full of amorous
fancies," but the fancies are only empty conceits that have no passion in their veins. The
sonnets of Dante Gabriel Rossetti come nearer
to the Italian model. It is true the women of
Verona used to point out the author of the
Divina Commedia and whisper: "Do you see
that man? that is he who goes down to hell
whenever he pleases and brings us back tidings
of the sinners below!" and the usual response
was: "Quite likely; his face is scarred with
fire and darkened with smoke, and his beard
and hair are singed." But Dante was a handsome youth when Beatrice Portinari, a child of
only eight years, won his heart. Not the fires
of hell, but persecution, banishment, and, most
of all, Gemma Donati gave him a sorrowful
countenance and austere manners. He wrote
the *Vita Nuova* in 1294, in the twenty-ninth
year of his age and four years after the death
of Beatrice, and the entire work glows with the
characteristic passion of the Italian sonnet.
The Earl of Lytton gives us, in the *Nineteenth
Century* for November, 1881, an epitome of
the *Vita Nuova*, which, though prepared in a
semi-humorous spirit, illustrates the peculiar

mingling of earthly passion and heavenly love
which characterizes the Italian sonnet:

Dante has a dream. In his dream he has seen a
lady sleeping in the arms of the god of love. She
is naked but for the partial clothing of a scarlet
scarf. The god in one arm encircles his companion; in the hand of the other he holds a lump of
flesh which he appears to have been cooking or
burning during her slumber. The poet, after careful contemplation of it, perceives that it is his own
heart in flames. The god then awakes the lady
and persuades her to eat the poet's grilled heart.
This she does with not unnatural reluctance; after
which the poet himself arranges and convokes a
council of poets for the full discussion of his dream,
as if it were a municipal question for the investigation of a syndicate. Having thus invited general
attention to that shyest and most strikingly sensitive of all moral conditions—a young man's first-
born and new-born love for a young woman—the
unbashful but wily bard affects a modest reluctance
to name the object of his passion, and resorts to a
ruse for the concealment of it, by celebrating the
charms of no less than sixty other ladies whom he
names. But the artifice is defeated by a miracle
no less artificial than its arithmetical puzzle, in
which the name of Beatrice always turns up ninth.
Why ninth? Ah, thereby hangs a tale. She was in
her ninth year when he saw her the first time, in her
eighteenth year when he saw her the second time,

and twice nine are eighteen. She died in the ninth
month of the Judaic year, when the century was
ten times nine years old. Which things are an allegory, showing that Beatrice was a nine. And
what is a nine? A miracle of which the root is the
Holy Trinity: three multiplied by itself."

We cannot follow the Earl of Lytton when
he tells us that "from beginning to end there
is not one note of genuine passion in it." We
should say of the *Vita Nuova*, it is in places
crowded with passion so incandescent at times
as to amount to religious fervor.

Two very perverse sonneteers are Cecco
Angiolieri and Folgore da San Geminiano.
Their passion is dark and malevolent. Cecco
is described by Rossetti, in his *Dante and His
Circle*, as "the prodigal or scamp of the Dantesque cycle." It is but just to say of Folgore's
muse that, evil-starred as it is, there is about
it a fresh and lovely spirit mingling with a
noble and chivalrous temper. We cannot prevent ourselves from loving the often perverse,
but always delicate, gentle, and yet sprightly
Folgore da San Geminiano. In a sonnet
addressed to God and filled with rage against
the Ghibellines, he shows us the ill-tempered
and impious side of his wayward muse:

"I praise thee not, O God, nor give thee glory,
    Nor yield thee any thanks, nor bow the knee,

Nor pay thee service; for this irketh me
More than the souls to stand in purgatory;
Since thou hast made us Guelphs a jest and story
Unto the Ghibellines for all to see: .
And if Uguccion claimed tax of thee,
Thou 'd t pay it without interrogatory.
Ah, well I wot they know thee! and have stolen
St. Martin from thee, Altopascio,
St. Michael, and the treasure thou hast lost;
And thou that rotten rabble so hast swollen
That pride now counts for tribute; even so
Thou 'st made their heart stone-hard to thine
own cost."

Here is a specimen of Cecco's good-humor and
kindly feeling:

"An I were fire, I would burn up the world;
An I were wind, with tempest I 'd it break;
An I were sea, I 'd drown it in a lake;
An I were God, to hell I 'd have it hurled;
An I were Pope, I 'd see disaster whirled
O'er Christendom, deep joy thereof to take;
An I were Emperor, I 'd quickly make
All heads of all folk from their necks be twirled;
An I were death, I 'd to my father go;
An I were life, forthwith from him I 'd fly;
And with my mother I 'd deal even so;
An I were Cecco, as I am but I,
Young girls and pretty for myself I 'd hold,
But let my neighbors take the plain and old."

The American sonnet strikes the happy medium, and is neither incandescent nor coldly ethical. It has the warmth of spring and not the torrid glow of summer. Paul H. Hayne gives us a beautiful sonnet called *October*. The sonnets of the gifted and unfortunate Henry Timrod are among the best our country has produced; they are pure in spirit, graceful in style, and full of the most delicate feeling. Thomas Bailey Aldrich has a remarkably delicate sonnet on *Sleep*:

"When to soft Sleep we give ourselves away,
 And in a dream as in a fairy bark
 Drift on and on through the enchanted dark
 To purple daybreak—little thought we pay
 To that sweet bitter world we know by day.
 We are clean quit of it, as is a lark
 So high in heaven no human eye may mark
 The thin swift pinion cleaving through the gray.
 Till we awake ill fate can do no ill,
 The resting heart shall not take up again
 The heavy load that yet must make it bleed;
 For this brief space the loud world's voice is
     still,
 No faintest echo of it brings us pain.
 How will it be when we shall sleep indeed?"

DANTE

MARIA FRANCESCA ROSSETTI, daughter of Gabriel Rossetti, an old Dantean commentator, has written a book called *A Shadow of Dante*. The volume is neat, elegantly conceived, and full of the richest thought. The frontispiece represents the bust of the poet "as Giotto painted it, as time altered it, and as shadow showed it," with the singularly expressive motto,

"Lo corpo dentro al quale io facea ombra."

The book consists of eleven chapters. The first is prefatory, the second is devoted to an account of Dante's universe, the third to his life-experience, and the remaining eight contain an analysis of the poem. Very little in the book is original, but everything is excellent. In the third chapter are discussed such questions as, Who or what was Dante's Beatrice? Was she a woman, or a conception of the imagination, or was she both? When did the poet first enter public life? Where was Dante and what was he doing in the critical period between the death of Beatrice, in 1290, and his meeting her in Paradise in the spring of 1300?

.It is well Miss Rossetti's book has been published, since of all poets there is none so thoroughly misunderstood as the author of the *Divina Commedia*. Six hundred years separate him from our century, but six thousand years separate him from our intellects.

Between Dante and Homer there is a certain unconscious and noble rivalry—the rivalry not of ambitions, but of natures. Homer is fragmentary—so fragmentary that some pronounce the *Iliad* to be the work of several authors. But no one can, in all the centuries to come, speak or think thus of the work of the great Italian poet. Through the *Divina Commedia* runs a consistency and continuity of purpose, strong enough to hold all the cantos in their right places and all the characters in their right cantos, and yet so gentle that the ethereal mysticism with which the poem is enveloped is undisturbed. Homer's poems are like great cities that have not crumbled nor decayed for centuries; but Dante's city is of one stone, and, like the Jerusalem of which John writes, "eternal in the heavens."

Dante has Homer's genius, but Homer has

not Dante's art. Homer is every inch the hero
—strong, massive, impersonal. His lines have
the ring of steel, and the canter of horses; they
hurl themselves at you like javelins. Dante
is the intellectual saint. Mystical but not ob-
scure, his lines are perfect light, and the vision
passes through them to their meaning. In
them light and sweetness, like sound and motion, mutually depend, and the warmth of love
does not melt the purity of virtue. Dante's
goodness has the touch of classicism. He
wrote in the light of a great conviction—the
conviction that all things were made for the
soul.

To many, Dante is the north pole of literature — grand, gloomy, desolate, and cold.
Their mistake arises from the fact that they
measure literature by their own firesides. The
warmth of social life is as different from the
warmth of literature as day from night. There
are as many flowers as flakes of snow in Dante's
poems. Dante is not the earth's pole; he is
the earth's orbit through which all zones whirl.
Men bewail the loneliness of his life and the
solitariness of his character; but it is their own
frivolousness that makes his heights and depths
lonely and gloomy. His companionship and
character may be beyond the range of their
observation, but they are not less real for that.

To those who find Dante cold, no comment will make him warm—their difficulty is organic. You might as well attempt to reshape a diamond with a pocket-knife as to cut him down to vulgar comprehension.

Dante makes the tour of hell and purgatory, and all the while his personal materiality is rendered apparent and clearly outlined by the shadowy presence of Virgil, his companion. The lost souls, in darkness and tormented, marvel that flesh and blood are there. Farinata lifts himself from his tomb of fire, and looks on the form of Dante. Francesca, filled with wonder and grief, hastens to tell her story of love and sorrow:

> "Poi mi rivolsi a loro, e parla' io,
> E cominciai: 'Francesca, i tuoi martìri
> A lagrimar mi fanno tristo e pio.
>
> Ma dimmi: al tempo de' dolci sospiri,
> A che, e come concedette Amore
> Che conosceste i dubbiosi desiri?'
>
> Ed ella a me: 'Nessun maggior dolore,
> Che ricordarsi del tempo felice
> Nella miseria; e ciò sa 'l tuo dottore.
>
> Ma s' a conoscer la prima radice
> Del nostro amor tu hai cotanto affetto,
> Farò come colui che piange e dice.
>
> Noi leggevamo un giorno per diletto
> Di Lancillotto, come amor lo strinse;

Soli eravamo e senza alcun sospetto.
  Per più fïate gli occhi ci sospinse
Quella lettura, e scolorocci 'l viso;
Ma solo un punto fu quel che ci vinse.
  Quando leggemmo il disïato riso
Esser baciato da cotanto amante,
Questi, che mai da me non fia diviso,
  La bocca mi baciò tutto tremante:
Galeotto fu il libro e chi lo scrisse;
Quel giorno più non vi leggemmo avante.'
  Mentre che l'uno spirto questo disse,
L'altro piangeva sì, che di pietade
Io venni men, così com' io morisse;
  E caddi come corpo morto cade.''

But with the loss of his personality he does not bid farewell to that "stirring realism" which he everywhere unites with a certain mysticism, and which followed him through hell and purgatory, and showed so fearfully in the terrible words written over the gate of the Abode of Woe, at the beginning of the third canto of the *Inferno* :

"Through me you pass into the grieving realm;
Through me you pass into the eternal grief;
Through me you pass among the kin that 's lost.
Justice impelled my Maker the All-High;
The Puïssance Divine created me,
The Supreme Wisdom, and the Primal Love.

Before myself, created things were not,
Unless eternal:—I eternal last.
Leave off all hope, all ye that enter in."
                              ROSSETTI's translation.

His sonnets have the same mystical realism
—this, for instance:

" A day agone, as I rode sullenly
    Upon a certain path that liked me not,
    I met Love midway while the air was hot,
Clothed lightly as a wayfarer might be.
And for the cheer he showed, he seemed to me
    As one who hath lost lordship he had got;
    Advancing tow'rds me full of sorrowful
        thought,
Bowing his forehead so that none should see.
Then as I went, he called me by my name,
    Saying: 'I journey since the morn was dim
    Thence where I made thy heart to be: which
        now
I needs must bear unto another dame.'
    Wherewith so much passed into me of him
    That he was gone, and I discerned not how."

There are souls that climb the mountain of
spiritual attainment, reach the summit, and
are there transfigured—such is Dante's. With
him the summit of the mountain is in the
thirty-first canto of the *Paradiso*, where he
finds that Beatrice has left him, and returned

to her throne. In that upper air and shadow-less light, his personality passes away, and he is dissolved in his own song, leaving music, nothing but music, where was the form, the color, and the stature of the man. The angel of this transfiguration is Beatrice. Dante gives us in the thirtieth canto of the *Paradiso*, this wonderful and dazzling description of the divine glory and light into which Beatrice leads him, and within which the saints and angels forever dwell:

" Lume è lassù, che visibile face,
    Lo Creatore a quella creatura,
    Che solo in lui vedere ha la sua pace;
E si distende in circular figura
    In tanto che la sua circonferenza
    Sarebbe al Sol troppo larga cintura.
Fassi di raggio tutta sua parvenza
    Reflesso al sommo del Mobile primo,
    Che prende quindi vivere e potenza;
E come clivo in acqua di suo imo
    Si specchia quasi per vedersi adorno
    Quando è nel verde e ne' fioretti opimo;
Sì soprastando al lume intorno intorno
    Vide specchiarsi in più di mille soglie
    Quanto da noi lassù fatto ha ritorno.
E se l' infimo grado in se raccoglie
    Sì grande lume, quant' è la larghezza
    Di questa rosa nell' estreme foglie?

8

La vista mia nell' ampio e nell' altezza
Non si smarriva, ma tutto prendeva
Il quanto e'l quale, di quell' allegrezza.
Presso e lontano lì, nè pon, nè leva;
Che dove Dio senza mezzo governa.
La legge natural nulla rilieva
Nel giallo della rosa sempiterna
Che si dilata rigrada, e redole
Odor di lode al Sol, che sempre verna,
Qual è colui, che tace e dicer vuole,
Mi trasse Beatrice."

In the *Vita Nuova* he sweetly sings of Beatrice:

" Love saith concerning her: 'How chanceth it
That flesh, which is of dust, should be thus
pure ?'
Then, gazing always, he makes oath: 'For sure
This is a creature of God till now unknown.'
She hath that paleness of a pearl that 's fit
In a fair woman, so much and not more;
She is as high as Nature's skill can soar;
Beauty is tried by her comparison.
Whatever her sweet eyes are turned upon,
Spirits of love do issue thence in flame,
Which through their eyes who then may look
on them
Pierce to the heart's deep chamber every one.
And in her smile Love's image you may see;
Whence none can gaze upon her steadfastly."

After her death he writes:

" Not by the frost of Winter was she driven
 Away, like others; nor by Summer heats;
 But through a perfect gentleness, instead.
 For from the lamp of her meek lowlihead
Such an exceeding glory went up hence
 That it woke wonder in the Eternal Sire,
 Until a sweet desire
Entered Him for that lovely excellence,
 So that He bade her to Himself aspire:
Counting this weary and most evil place
Unworthy of a thing so full of grace."

A Beatrice Portinari nel vi *Centenario della sua Morte le Donne Italiane* may be a beautiful book, and a suitable memorial of the lovely daughter of Folco Portinari; it may be also a graceful tribute from the ladies of Italy, and especially from Carlotta Ferrari, to whose enterprise we are indebted for the existence of the work; and it may go well with the bust presented to Florence; but no earthly Beatrice is celebrated in the *Convito* and *Divina Commedia*, whatever may be the nature of the loved one honored in the *Vita Nuova*. In the *Convito* Beatrice is described as Philosophy:

"I, who sought to console myself, found not only a remedy for my tears, but words of authors and of sciences and of books; reflecting on which I judged well that Philosophy, who was the Lady of these authors, of these sciences, and of these books, might be a supreme thing. And I imagined her in the form of a gentle Lady; and I could imagine her in no other attitude than a compassionate one, because if willingly the sense of Truth beheld her, hardly could it turn away from her. And with this imagination I began to go where she is demonstrated truthfully, that is, to the Schools of the Religious, and to the disputations of the Philosophers; so that in a short time, perhaps of thirty months, I began to feel her sweetness so much that my love for her chased away and destroyed all other thought.''

This Philosophy is the transfiguration of his first love; the ideal of his innermost spiritual nature, all of which is conveyed to us in the name of the celestial Lady, Beatrice—*source of beatitude*. A young and beautiful maiden may have wedded Simone de' Bardi, and may have adorned his home with her earthly presence for a few brief years; but it is only in the exalted and pure mind of the poet that she becomes the ''fountain of all truth'' and the ''splendor of eternal light.'' So far as concerns us, this heavenly Lady is no woman at all, but the uplifting and inspiring womanly element; she is Divine Philosophy consuming the earthly in the heavenly love. And thus at last must all earthly love be changed into something more ethereal, that it may survive the mutation of years and the dust of death; its mortal must put on immortality, and then only shall Death be swallowed up in victory.

Great as is Dante's immortal poem, still it is not a poem of human tenderness and compassion. We are charmed by its mingled gentleness and power, but we never come upon anything resembling deep sympathy with the human heart in its inward sorrow and daily burden.

" Ah! from what agonies of heart and brain,
　　What exultations trampling on despair,
　　　　What tenderness, what tears, what hate of
　　　　wrong,
　　What passionate outcry of a soul in pain
　　　Uprose this poem of the earth and air,
　　　　This mediæval miracle of song!"
　　　　　　　　　　　　　LONGFELLOW.

There may have been "agonies of heart and brain," and there may have been "tears" and "hate of wrong," but we have always felt that "tenderness" had little to do with the making of the *Divina Commedia*. There is decided want of anything like human feeling in both the face of Dante as Giotto transmits it, and in the great poem itself. The *Inferno* is twice more infernal than any other hell of which we have knowledge, whether it be in tradition, art, or literature. Within its depths of unutterable horror are imprisoned forever real men and women, "bone of our bone and flesh of our flesh," whose misery and shame awaken no sentiment of compassion in the implacably righteous heart of the creator of that "mediæval miracle of song." Virgil, from whom we should have expected less, since he was not suckled at the breasts of the Beatitudes, looked upon the awful scene with gentler, sadder, and more compassionate vision. The *Divina Commedia* is one of the greatest of all poetic compositions; it is full of the most earnest religious feeling; it has a tremendous moral power; moreover, there are in it suggestions of exquisite grace, and infinite depths of longing and aspiration not altogether untouched by the most fervent passion; but it certainly displays little of the tenderness that perceives the pathos of man's life on earth, and the mystery of the vast future that awaits him.

Mr. Head, whose privately printed book, *Studies in Mediæval and Modern History*, is well worth the reading, thinks that Dante took bribes, or, as he expresses it, "boodle." If Mr. Head is right, what shall be said of Maz-

zini's statement: "Dante kept himself faithful
to his God, to his purpose, to himself.   Nothing could bend or corrupt his soul.   It was like
the diamond, which can only be conquered by
its own dust.''

Without possessing private knowledge of the
matter, we venture a suggestion that the charge
of dishonesty made against Dante was not
wholly free from political purpose and feeling.
Further, we have a suspicion that Dante was in
reality *technically* dishonest in some of his relations to public affairs; and yet we are sure that
he did not intend to defraud any one.   He
was a politician as well as a poet; and was associated with, and in some degree responsible
for the "wire-pulling" of five hundred years
ago.   We think Mazzini's words are true in
every way, and yet we are by no means sure
that Dante could have defended in every respect his own political career.

DANTE'S DOCTRINE THAT CON-
CEALS ITSELF

"O ye who have undistempered intellects,
Observe the doctrine that conceals itself
Beneath the veil of mysterious verses!"

Inferno, ix., 61.

LONGFELLOW, commenting upon these
lines, tells us that "the doctrine that
conceals itself" is that negation or unbelief
is a gorgon's head which turns the human
heart into stone; after which

"No more returning upward can there be."

The spirit of destruction is the spirit that
denies—denies for the sake of denying. It is
better to believe the fairy-tales of childhood
than, discarding these, to abandon with them
faith in truth. When we have parted from
confidence in the divine veracity, we have surrendered every adequate motive for noble
thinking and living. When we have brought
ourselves through vain philosophy and "science

falsely so-called" to distinguish no difference between good and evil, and have learned to say to evil, "Be thou my good!" then has the gorgon's head of unbelief changed the yielding heart into unfeeling stone, and rendered impossible all "returning upward." When the intellect announces to man's spiritual nature that one is at liberty to believe what pleases him, and that it is a matter of no consequence to what conclusions he may arrive, the spiritual nature is in most cases ready to respond, "I believe in nothing." There remains to be taken but one more mental step, and that is the conversion of negation into a philosophical system. Such conversion we have in Schopenhauer's pessimism and von Hartmann's exposition of the doctrine of the innate evil of all things which Edgar Saltus has called "The Philosophy of Disenchantment." In the sense in which philosophy is love of wisdom, and science is classified knowledge, disenchantment with God, His creatures, and His works can never belong to either; but as an investigation into the causes of phenomena, the disenchantment may bring forward some plausible claim to a place in ratiocination. It cannot become a real philosophy according to etymology, because it does not love; and it cannot become a science because it does not know. It may be called philosophy in the sense of systematic argumentation, but the process of reasoning must be downward. One does not have to read *The Anatomy of Negation* to see that unbelief is the gorgon's head that changes the heart into stone. Doubt may lead the soul to truth if there be within it honesty and a pure desire for light, but the scornful spirit that, like a mocking devil, shatters the idol for the mere pleasure that comes of destruction, and that wantonly pours contempt upon truth and all those higher hopes and aspirations which spring from the love of it, is nigh unto perdition. The man who, believing in nothing, has learned to exult in his own spiritual failure, and to boast of his soul's emptiness, has sealed the doom of his own heart, and upon that stony tablet the finger of the Unseen is swiftly writing: "*Mene, mene, tekel, upharsin.*"

DANTE'S THREE LADIES

" Three ladies at the right wheel in a circle
Came around dancing; one so very red
That in the fire she hardly had been noted.
The second was as if her flesh and bones
Had all been fashioned out of emerald;
The third appeared as snow but newly fallen."
Purgatorio, xxix., 121.

THE three ladies or nymphs represent the
three Christian virtues or graces, charity,
hope, and faith.

Charity was "very red." The ruby signified
divine love, the Holy Spirit, the creative power,
and royalty. In an evil sense it stood for war,
murder, and anger. In the East the ruby is a
symbol of wine and sensual pleasures; thus
Hafiz makes use of it in a characteristic stanza:

"A double ruby is my fascinating ruin;
Long time ago their fatal charm my bosom flew in.
Whate'er resisting reason says, quite vanquished
    mine is:
One ruby is thy luring mouth, the other mine is."[1]

[1] Alger, *Poetry of the Orient.*

Dante's red lady was the Charity ("Love" in I Corinthians xiii., revised version) of the New Testament. The apostle Paul pronounces it the crowning grace of the Christian character. "Now abideth faith, hope, charity, these three; and the greatest of these is charity."

It is natural that the most exalted of graces should have for its emblem one of the most valuable of all precious stones. The ruby ranks above the sapphire, of which it is a variety. It differs from that stone in color only. It may be the glowing and ardent nature of love, which we instinctively describe as a flame, and which has been represented as a tongue of fire resting upon a human heart, accounts for the choice of the ruby.

Hope "was as if her flesh and bones had all been fashioned out of emerald." The emerald as a symbol of spring stood for hope—especially the hope of immortality, which the early flowers bring before us in their suggestions of the resurrection. The emerald stood also for victory, which was signified in the green color of palm and laurel. The emerald, with its bright velvety green, is still held in high regard by Eastern monarchs. It is in Oriental courts the imperial stone because of its color. Ancient Hindus represented the chariot of the sun as drawn by seven green horses. Nero, who was near-sighted, watched gladiatorial combats through an eye-glass of emerald. Faith "appeared as snow but newly fallen." The diamond represented pure white light— chastity, virginity, and life. It was also a sign of integrity. The white robe of the judge symbolized justice. The rich adopted white as an emblem of humility. Women wore it as a sign of chastity, hence it was a color ever sacred to the Virgin Mary, who was dressed in white in all the old pictures of the Assumption. In the zodiac the diamond belongs to Virgo.

Did Dante desire to show forth the Holy Trinity in the three ladies or Christian graces? Charity, with its ruby-red flame, reminds us of the Creator, who calls Himself "Our Heavenly Father," and who, from love of the world, gave His only begotten Son to save that world from the guilt and penalty of sin. God is love —that is, charity, as the New Testament in its ordinary translation uses the word. Hope, "that was as if her flesh and bones had all been fashioned out of emerald," calls up before our vision the picture of the Saviour who brought to sinful man the blessed hope of immortality. He illustrated that hope by Himself rising like the flowers in spring-time from the grave. Do not the emerald-green palm and

laurel speak to our hearts of His victory over
the winter-world of death?   Faith, pure as the
newly-fallen snow, represents to us the un-
created Light of God — the Holy Spirit.
Chastity, justice, and humility all point to
the third person in the Godhead.   White was
the Virgin Mary's color, because it stood for
chastity.   She bore a Son whose immaculate
conception was the work of the Holy Spirit.

The Hindus were not astray when they gave
the horses of the sun the color of an emerald.
Our Saviour is represented in the Bible as a
sun the divine rays of which are destined to
illuminate the entire world with the blessed
spring-time doctrine of the resurrection.   Of
God's Son it is said that His kingdom (green
palms and laurels of victory) shall cover the
earth.   Our thoughts naturally turn to Charles
Tennyson Turner's exquisite sonnet on

THE HOLY EMERALD.

Said to be the only true likeness of Christ.

" The gem to which the artist did intrust
    That face which now outshines the cherubim,
  Gave up, full willingly, its emerald dust,
    To take Christ's likeness, to make room for
      Him.
So must it be, if thou would'st bear about

Thy Lord — thy shining surface must be
    low'red,
Thy goodly prominence be chipt and scored,
Till those deep scars have brought His features
   . out:
Sharp be the stroke and true, make no com-
    plaints;
  For heavenly life thou givest earthly grit;
But oh! how oft our coward spirit faints,
  When we are called our jewels to submit
  To this keen graver, which so oft hath writ
The Saviour's image on His wounded saints! "

LATER ITALIAN NOTES

DANTE, *Vita Nuova*, xxxv. : "*Nel ciel dell' umiltate ov' è Maria,*" but Dante's "humility" was tranquillity — that Divine Peace which is an equal blessing to high and low. He thought it was in the empyrean, which, he tells us, resembles "the Divine Science" (*Convito*, ii., 15); and, indeed, that only is the true empyrean which hath serenity of knowledge. Our earthly wisdom is full of battle and unrest, but the "Divine Science" is full of all peace—that peace "which suffers no strife of opinions or sophistical arguments, because of the exceeding certitude of its subject, which is God." In God is neither doubt nor argument. "The calm heaven where Mary hath her home" (Norton's translation) is calm because of the "exceeding certitude"; and the certitude is because of God. Therefore, only in God can man, made in the Divine Image, have rest.

"Who God possesseth
In nothing is wanting;
Alone God sufficeth."

" Now say to Fra Dolcino, then, to arm him,
Thou, who perhaps wilt shortly see the sun,
If soon he wish not here to follow me,
So with provisions, that no stress of snow
May give the victory to the Novarese,
Which otherwise to gain would not be easy."
                                    Inferno, xxviii.

Such was the message Dante was commissioned to bring up from the under world.
Notwithstanding all that has been written against Fra Dolcino and his "Apostles," it is very clear that he lived the life of a good man and died the death of a martyr. He was mistaken in some matters, but his main purpose was to bring the Roman Church back to the simplicity of primitive faith. He was burned at the stake with his brave companion, the beautiful Margaret of Trent, at Vercelli, in 1307.

" My Master, much should I be pleased,
If I could see him soused into this broth,
Before we issue forth out of the lake.

. . . .

A little after that, I saw such havoc
Made of him by the people of the mire
That still I praise and thank my God for it."
                                    Inferno, viii.

We know nothing about Filippo Argenti
beyond the little that is gleaned from the un-
generous page of Dante and a few words in
Boccaccio.   It is more than likely he was as
the latter poet represents him: "A man of
great wealth and of a wonderful strength.   It
is said that his horse was shod with silver, and
that he lived like a prince.   He was an unjust
man, and of a furious temper."   It is not surprising that the poet hated a brutal and vulgar
tyrant; and we do not need to be told of family
and political reasons for the delight that swelled
the heart of Dante when he saw such havoc
made of Filippo Argenti by the people of the
mire.   But in the *Inferno* lines we discern
something more than the indignation of a
righteous man.   In them we have a beautiful
and typical exhibition of that peculiar vehemence of feeling and expression which appears
to be an inherent element of Italian mind and
literature.   We have the same thing in Cecco
Angiolieri and Folgore da San Geminiano.
Their passion is no doubt dark and malevolent;
and Cecco is precisely what Rossetti calls him:
"the prodigal or scamp of the Dantesque
cycle"; but the vehemence of these two is
common to all.

I cannot see why the relation Alfieri sus-

tained to the Countess of Albany should so
greatly disturb the minds of readers of Italian
verse. The poet and the lady may have been
married in law, and certainly they were wedded
in heart and life. She was the inspiration of
his genius, and all the world owes her a debt
of gratitude. It may be the Abate Caluso,
who was with Alfieri in his last hours, and who
placed the hand of the widow of Charles Edward Stuart in that of the dying poet, and
who, later, wrote the epitaph that adorns the
monument,—it may be that he knew all about
the matter, which certainly does not concern
us. If he did he was a wise, discreet, and right-
minded man who knew enough to take the
secret with him into his grave. An author's
books when once published belong to the
world, but his private life remains his own. It
does not follow that because a poet's work interests others, he must dress and undress after
the fashion of old-time kings, in a crowded
room. If Alfieri's life was immoral, what
shall be said of the even more vicious curiosity
of a public that delights to dwell upon every
detail, and resorts to imagination when facts
are wanting?

JACOPONE DA TODI

JACOPONE DA TODI sold all he had, and distributed to the poor; he entered gay and thoughtless society with his naked body harnessed in the trappings of an ass; he consumed ten years in most abject self-abasement; he made himself to appear in the eyes of his fellow-men "entirely hideous, vile, and stinking, beyond the most abominable carrion"—all this he did for the glory of God and the development of his own spiritual nature. We laugh at his grotesque penance, almost insane misuse of himself, and absurd view of the divine requirements; we lounge in our easy chairs, and congratulate ourselves upon the possession of a superior wisdom which renders faith and practice reasonable and moderate. We seldom reflect that Jacopone and his brother saints were, notwithstanding all their errors and superstitions, men of deep religious feeling and exalted piety. Can we always

compare without shame our light-encircled
lives with the darkened lives of mediæval
saints? Is not our increase in culture marked
by some decrease in faith? With the reason
one may discover duty; with the will he may
force himself into external obedience to its requirements; but only with the heart can he so
love "I ought" as to change it into "I desire."
The Pillar Saints are to be commended not
for what they did, but for what they sought to
do, since aspiration rather than attainment is
the true measure of character. Thus viewed,
Jacopone, the Pillar Saints, and a large number of the persecutors and fanatics of the Dark
Ages were men of a piety which as greatly
dwarfs our colorless twentieth-century belief
as do the giant trees of California the stunted
shrubs of the far North. Without warmth of
emotion there can be no large display of self-
sacrifice, and where self-sacrifice is wanting religion itself, save as a cold abstraction, must
be wanting also. Jacopone's life may have
resembled that of a madman, and it is more
than likely he was at times entirely out of his
mind, but no one who understands the spirit
that moved within him, and certainly no one
who is acquainted with his poems, can fail of
seeing that he was a simple-hearted and noble-
minded man.

Jacopone da Todi was no blind follower of other men, though he was the natural outcome of a system within the limits of which he lived and died. He had his own ideas of the very papacy of which he was the creature, and against its great corruptions he lifted up his voice in no uncertain tones. He was as courageous to rebuke a wicked Pope as he was ready to denounce a low-born thief. He likened Boniface VIII. to a fox, a wolf, and a dog, and being confined in a loathsome dungeon for his frankness, broke forth into singing. Some of his best literary work was wrought in the silence and solitude of a prison. As the Hebrew prophet was from the people and for the people, so was Jacopone's heart with the poor and oppressed. He was a prophet of the people, ever fearless to plead the cause of the distressed against the greed and cruelty of the wealthy and powerful. The gay and careless children of feasting and revelry might laugh at his sour countenance and severe penance, but the fatherless and widows found in him a faithful friend, and upon his head descended the blessings of many who, lowly born and unprotected, received from him the helpful and tender ministrations of a beautiful Christian charity.

For the mingling of pure spiritual feeling

with intense passion, few specimens of literature can be compared with the verses of
Jacopone da Todi. Read *La Poesie spirituali
del Beato Jacopone da Todi*—that is, if you have
the patience to wade through one thousand
and fifty-five closely printed pages—and you
will find yourself bewildered, delighted, and re-
pelled by a work which, while it challenges
admiration, makes heart and brain faint as
from the overpowering odor of hundreds of
cut flowers in a closed room. You rise from
the perusal of *Spiritual Love Songs, Penitential
Hymns,* and *Spiritual Secrets* with a feeling of
distress and of partial intoxication. The soul
seems to be under the strange influence of a
spell that, while it bathes the imagination in
bliss, binds its limbs that it cannot rise, and
clips its wings that it cannot soar. As the
most welcome anæsthetic at first repels with a
sense of asphyxia, so these wonderful poems,
from which we afterward derive so much
pleasure, have for their first effect a very decided feeling of discomfort. Your first impulse
is to throw wide open the window and draw
into the lungs a deep breath of cool fresh air.
And yet after the sense of suffocation is gone,
you return to the book and re-enter that
"realm of ecstacy" with new delight. One cannot in this climate and age long contemplate

without some spiritual discomfort lines like
these:

" Love, love, thou hast me smitten, wounded sore!
No speech but love, love, love, can I deliver!
Love, I am one with thee, to part no more!
Love, love, thee only shall I clasp forever!
Love, love, strong love, thou forcest me to soar
Heavenward! my heart expands; with love I
    quiver;
For thee I swoon and shiver,
Love, apart with thee to dwell!
Love, if thou lovest me well,
Oh, make me die of love!

" Love, love, love, Jesus, I have scaped the seas!
Love, love, love, Jesus, thou hast guided me!
Love, love, love, Jesus, give me rest and peace!
Love, love, love, Jesus, I 'm inflamed by thee!
Love, love, love, Jesus! From wild waves re-
    lease!
Make me, love, dwell forever clasped with thee,
And be transformed in thee,
In truest charity,
In highest verity
Of pure transmitted love! " [1]

These verses are cold and expressionless
in comparison with other lines in this wonderful *Hymn of Divine Love ;* there are lines so

[1] Symond's translation.

incandescent that we shrink from turning them
into English.   It must be remembered that
northern and southern temperaments are as
widely separated in religious feeling and expression as in the externals of ordinary life.
The very air of Italy is voluptuous, and all
the associations of art, as well as the habits
and manners of the people, tend in the same
direction.   The religious life is no exception.
We have it from an Italian that "men sang
the same *strambotti* to the Virgin and the lady
of their love, to the Rose of Jericho and the
red rose of the balcony."   Love was to them
one and the same thing, whether it flamed up
to heaven or found its way into the heart of
an earthly mistress.   And yet the author of
Stabat Mater Dolorosa was no languid, mystical,
and voluptuous visionary; he could strike
heavy blows at great evils, and write strong
lines full of warning and rebuke.   The sorrows
of lost souls in hèll and the terrors of the
Judgment Day were among his themes, and he
displayed as great fertility of genius in dealing
with these as in describing the marriage of
the Christ with the soul of the believer.

THE AMULET OF PASCAL

DR. ELAM (in *A Physician's Problems*) explains the Amulet of Pascal by assuming that the wonderful man had in "the year of grace 1654, Monday, the 23d of November," a vision of a globe of fire upon which was stamped the mark of the cross, which globe and cross were to him a sure sign that his salvation was accomplished. Our medical author may be right, and yet the more we think upon it the more it seems to us that another explanation is at least possible. Why may not the amulet have been a reminder of peril by fire, against which the gifted philosopher and mathematician was to guard himself "from about half-past ten in the evening until half-past twelve?" No doubt Pascal was very religious, and we know that in his parchment packet were sundry ecstatic and devout ejaculations; but he was also what would have been called, even in his own day, superstitious. He had written FIRE in large letters; but never had he spoken of the matter, and it was only after his death that the inscription was found. He dwelt alone in the cloister of Port Royal, communing at frequent intervals with Arnauld, Le Saci, and other Jansenist writers, and contemplating the great problems of mathematics and mental science. He brooded over the vast unknown; dreamed dreams and saw visions; and these took color from the splendor of an intellect that could astonish Descartes with a work on Conic Sections from a youth of sixteen, and later delight the world, and ruin the Order of Loyola, with *Provincial Letters* that Voltaire did not hesitate to place by the side of the best works of Molière and Bossuet. It would not be a strange thing in such a man to think himself the special charge of Heaven, and to hold himself warned by a miracle of impending danger that was to be looked for "from about half-past ten in the evening until half-past twelve." It is the office of an amulet to afford magical or supernatural protection to the wearer; and it seems to us that Pascal viewed and used the little parchment, covered over with curious and mystical formulæ, as a warning and defence against a fire that was always burning before his brilliant and erratic imagination.

THE CATHOLICITY OF CULTURE

NOT to the finest intellectual perception joined to the largest knowledge of things, not to the *éducation de luxe* of the university, nor yet to the most acute and critical literary discernment are the noblest minds aspiring and working. The one great purpose and end of all attainment is nothing less than that rounded and wholesome culture which is no mere empty parade of fastidious tastes and selfish refinements of feeling, but is in every sense the development of the man himself. The end of all culture is life. The education that terminates in a science or an art is but superficial. Only when training, of whatever kind it may be, sinks into the man and becomes a part of his personality is there in his life the unfolding of possibilities and development of character that bring to human nature its richest and most beautiful reward. Not to know but to be, is the sublime end of all true education.

Acquaintance with some branch of learning is not to be confused with culture. There are hundreds of brilliant specialists who are in no true sense of the word cultivated. Nor is culture to be confounded with refinement of taste and manner. One does not have it because his perceptions are acute and his mental touch delicate. Certainly culture has nothing to do with the unlovely spirit of caste, with its calm indifference to the conditions and rights of others. There is nothing that bears the slightest resemblance to culture in the "our circle" spirit which always marks its possessor as a person of narrow outlook and conventional feeling. There can be no affinity between culture and priggishness. Culture is essentially catholicity and breadth of sympathy. Whatever a man may or may not have, having these, he is a cultivated man. With enlarged vision he takes in the diversities, and with sympathetic touch he lays hold of the countless relationships of the great world by which he is surrounded, and of which he is a part. Culture is cosmopolitan. The man of affairs equally with the man of books may have this fine and noble quality, but no narrow sectarian or selfish partisan can lay just claim to its exquisite grace and beauty. No one can live in "our little Zion" without being provincial. Nothing is more vulgar than sectarianism. Only as we know men and the world sympathetically, and

entertain the large fellowship of our race, are
we delivered from the belittling egotism of
small minds. Little minds go about to establish this or that creed and to proselyte in the
interests of this or that religious system, vainly,
yet franticly, imagining that Almighty God
has crammed into some little compend of doctrine or into some narrow denominational
enclosure all the wisdom of the ages. With
larger vision comes some measure of culture,
and a better understanding of the vast universe
of which man is but a part. Strife for victory
gives place to heavenly aspiration. The Sunday ritual and the Monday conventionality are
put aside, and the man rises to a nobler manhood. Once he lived by rule and thought
what others thought, but now he lives his own
life and is glad.

John of Salisbury has left it on record that
he thought the physicians of his day narrow
and opinionated. They knew so little that
they were sure they knew it all. He represented them as pompous, owl-like, and given
to grave shakings of the head. In all this he
was simply saying, "These men are provincial
and narrow; they are without catholicity."
We are not concerned with the question
whether the old-time doctors were or were
not as our critic has represented them, but we

are interested to see what so discerning a mind
thought of shallow pretence, and of that pedan-
tic assumption of wisdom which marks the high
tide of vulgarity. A modern physician, writing
in the *Lancet*, brings very much the same
charge against his own medical associates:

"Strip us of our respectability and we cannot as
a herd be told from a crowd of deacons of Little
Bethel — the same smugness, the same lack of
humor, the same worship of the sacred Mrs.
Grundy, the same fear of overstepping the stupid
little laws and customs which prevail among the
ignorant middle classes of our country districts."

But other professions are open to the same
reproach. The priest, Romish or Protestant,
who, consumed of his own ecclesiasticism, can
see neither God nor man apart from the rubrics
of his sect, in the interest of which he un-
churches all the rest of the Christian world, is
not one whit better than the physician of John
of Salisbury's time. He may be sure that he
is of the Apostolic Succession, but, nevertheless, his lack of catholicity and want of sympathy mark him as narrow and shallow; and
his technical knowledge of conventional religion by no means saves him from the reproach
of being an uncultivated and provincial man.
Only as we enter into other lives are we saved

from the belittling influence of selfishness.   In understanding others we come to understand ourselves.   Self-righteousness and self-complacency blind us to the good there is in others, and render us ridiculous in the eyes of men and women of true culture and real discernment.   Cowper has given us these lines:

" Ceremony leads her bigots forth,
  Prepared to fight for shadows of no worth;
  While truths on which eternal things depend
  Find not, or hardly find, a single friend.
  As soldiers watch the signal of command,
  They learn to bow, to kneel, to sit, to stand;
  Happy to fill religion's vacant place
  With hollow form, and gesture, and grimace."

The poet's picture brings before us a provincial mind.   It shows us a man lacking in outlook, narrow in sympathy, and wanting in true culture.   It brings before us a sectarian in all the hard unloveliness of his self-complacency. As presenting a welcome contrast to Cowper's sketch, we turn to these graceful words that describe Newman Hall, than whom there have been few nobler men upon our earth:

" His theology is the theology of Calvary.   Himself a nominal Congregationalist, he uses the Church of England liturgy in his Sunday services; he has

a Presbyterian board of elders; he assimilates with
Methodists in many of his modes of labor; he is
equally at home with Episcopalians like Bickersteth
or with Quakers like Bevan Braithwaite.   Dr. Hall
touches human life at many points.   He has been
the intimate associate of such leading minds as
John Bright, Dean Stanley, and Mr. Gladstone; he
walked in Westminster Abbey as one of the pall-
bearers of Lady Augusta Stanley, with dukes and
' lord bishops;'' he has entertained Gladstone at his
table.   At the same time he is one of the most attractive street preachers to the humblest poor on
the Surrey side of London.''

FORGOTTEN AMERICAN POETS

THERE lies upon the table in my library an engraving of "Eminent Living Poets" who were known to the American public half a century ago. The poets whose portraits adorn the engraving are Halleck, Bryant, Pinkney, Percival, Sprague, Brooks, Pierpont, Woodworth, and Washington Irving. All these were true sons of song in the opinion of Mr. James Eddy and the New York *Mirror* for 1827, but no one remembers much about them now. Halleck lives in a single stanza of *Marco Bozzaris*. Pinkney's "I fill this cup to one made up" is not without merit, but it is the only contribution that gives him any claim upon the remembrance of mankind. Percival made some pretty rhymes in his day, but long ago he took up his abode in the shadowy limbo of oblivion, where he patiently awaits the coming of good Mr. Markham of *The Man with the Hoe*, and more poets of his kind. Sprague and Brooks are names that awaken no echo. Pierpont is with us still in a few good hymns. Woodworth is forgiven his doggerel and permitted the asylum of everlasting silence for the sake of the little that was really good in *The Old Oaken Bucket*. Irving remains glorious in his prose, but as a poet, in the usual sense of the word, he never lived at all. *Sic transit gloria mundi*, all of which means in plain English, "What's the use?" The passing of these "Eminent Living Poets" will hardly dampen the aspirations of new singers, for every day brings its own fresh hope. Bryant is with difficulty kept alive by *Thanatopsis* and *The Death of the Flowers*, but the "gifted boys" and "sweet girl graduates" are sure of firmer ground and are of a more robust constitution. The sons of Harvard, Yale, Princeton, and a hundred more institutions of learning, must twang the harp-string long enough to find out what measure, if any, of poetical genius they possess; but when once the "aching void" has been discovered why not fill it up with something better than jingling rhymes? What this world most wants is high and noble living. Literature and all the arts are for life and the world, and are of value only as they serve the age and render our earthly homes more wholesome and inviting. We need men and women who by their very presence with us introduce a spirit of true chivalry, and not of mock-heroics; and who add to the finest feeling and the largest enthusiasm for humanity a strong and realistic hold upon an otherwise dull and mercenary world.

THE TANNERY AT MOUDON

IT may be there was really nothing dreadful in the Tannery at Moudon, where, according to Montgaillard, the skins of lords and ladies of France were tanned to make breeches and boots for "the People"—that is to say, the skins of such as were worth flaying. The Red Nightcaps of '93 were frugal—quite too economical in every way to waste the aristocratic material furnished by the "national razor." We of these Christianized and enlightened American States turn to no account the plebian stuff provided by our well-regulated gibbets and electric chairs, unless we take into consideration the "dissecting-bees" furnished to physicians by the State of New York. And yet we are not so prodigal after all, for in our Empire State there is a gentleman who announces that he can furnish to those who have a fancy for such articles a pair of slippers made entirely of human skin, for which he will charge only the modest sum of seven dollars. For the still more modest sum of three dollars he can sell a set of dice carved out of men's bones. If you represent a secret society, he has for you a skull, the eye-sockets of which are rendered luminous by incandescent lamps under red or green glass. We do not know what prices were commanded by the French Revolutionary leathers of a century ago, but Montgaillard says with the assurance of one who understands such matters: "Most of the hides taken from the ladies and little children were of so soft a texture as to be of little value;" but it must be remembered that thousands of people of both sexes and all ages were " looking through the little window, and sneezing into the sack." There must have been great variety, and no doubt the Tannery at Moudon turned out some fine specimens of work. Men have different integuments, but human nature is the same thing all the world over. What is made of it in one place can be made of it in another. Our American Judge Lynch (may the shade of honest James Lynch of 1688 forgive us) is not much better, and, perhaps, not much worse than "Attorney-General-of-the-Lamp-post" Desmoulins. Was not the negro Hoose cut up alive, saturated with oil, and burned while Southern gentlemen fought in the spirit of such chivalry as they knew of for skin-relics, and particles of bone?

Judge Lynch could dispose of ten and thirty
negroes burned alive on the other side of Mason
and Dixon's line in the year 1899. I doubt
not he could have given De Quincey some very
interesting and suggestive points on "Murder
Considered as one of the Fine Arts." When
the French Revolution is brought to mind it
should not be forgotten that there were in
America such places as Libby, Belle Isle, Dan-
ville, Salisbury, Charleston, and Andersonville
prisons. In the last-named prison there were
at one time more than thirty thousand Union
soldiers, crowded, smitten by the hot sun,
flooded with filthy water, exposed to the bullets
of brutal guards who shot at the prisoners in
wanton sport, and starved into skeletons. The
total number of prisoners received at Andersonville was about fifty thousand, of whom
twenty-five thousand died of exposure, starva-
tion, and cruelty. Henry Wirz, who was
appointed by General Winder to be superin-
tendent of all that wretchedness, kept nine
bloodhounds in his hut, between the stockade
and the graveyard, with which to hunt down
prisoners who should attempt to escape.
Fouquier Tinville with his "Batches," driving
the over-worked Samson distracted, was not
one whit worse than the Swiss-American
Wirz, with his twenty-five thousand human

beings starved to death or run down by bloodhounds.

So far back as 1835 this same spirit was alive
in these American States.   There was then in
our free republic a good and noble man from
England, George Thompson, who spoke and
worked against human slavery.   He helped
and advocated every worthy enterprise.   He
had compassion for the suffering.   He went
about like Jesus Christ with his hand out-
stretched to every son and daughter of calamity and distress.   He imperilled his own life
in keeping open the "underground railroad to
Canada."   His life was aglow with enthusiasm
for humanity.   The men of Massachusetts rose
up and mobbed him in the streets of Boston;
and he fared no better in Concord, N. H.
There was in New England a public offer of
one thousand dollars for the ears of George
Thompson.   When he was to lecture in Boston
a vessel was waiting to carry him to the South,
if the following placard, posted all over the
town, should result in his seizure:

"THOMPSON, THE ABOLITIONIST.

" That infamous foreign scoundrel, Thompson,
will hold forth this afternoon at 46 Washington
Street.   The present is a fair opportunity for the
friends of the Union to snake Thompson out.   It

will be a contest between the Abolitionists and the
friends of the Union. A purse of *one hundred
dollars* has been raised by a number of patriotic
citizens to reward the individual who shall first lay
violent hands on Thompson, so that he may be
brought to the tar-kettle before dark. Friends of
the Union, be vigilant! "

Differences in skin there may be, but human
nature is the same, and out of it you can
make both France and America; and in both
of these something worse, and also much better, than slippers and dice. Nôman-al-Aŝuar,
king of Hirah, is said to have cast Sennámar,
the architect, headlong from the highest tower
of the palace, to prevent him from ever building another structure so grand and costly; but
is a modern mining company any better than
was the old-time despot, when it sacrifices a
hundred lives to save new and improved
machinery? The Turkish Government encourages the massacre of Armenian Christians; but
is this western republic any better than the
"Sick Man of the East," when it permits the
slaughter of Chinese upon the Pacific Coast,
Indian outrages, and the burning of live
negroes at the South? Italy taxes her citizens, a large per cent of whom are paupers,
so oppressively that few have ever been able
to lift themselves from want to wealth; but is

England, in the tribute she exacts of Egypt,
better than her Latin sister of "arched and
lovely foot?" Is Massachusetts, with her
double taxation, more virtuous that was Spain
in Cuba or Portugal in Southeast Africa?
Human nature is the same in Turkey, England, Italy, Spain, Portugal, and the United
States; and out of it we can make the hideous
thing that was Nero, and all the worth and
nobleness we name Washington. We must be
patient if we would bring this encircling nature
of ours to any good result; and we can well
afford to bear with its failures and monstrosities
when we consider that we ourselves are a part
of its texture, and are involved in its unfolding.
Some one has written a book on the study
of astronomy through an opera-class—study
history through the lens of human nature, and
some of the most perplexing mysteries become
clear as noonday. In each man is all that was
base in Judas, Catiline, and Benedict Arnold;
fierce in Attila (*Flagellum Dei*); relentless in
the Spanish Inquisitors; vile in Henry VIII.;
and unbelievingly voluptuous in Leo X.; and
in each man as well is all that was sweetly devout in the Beloved John; steadfast in the
martyr host; noble in Luther; and sternly
righteous in the Fathers of New England.
Not only is each man "heir of all the ages,"

but child of the entire race.   The blood of all
is in each.   Only as we remember our common
root, and look out upon history through what
we know of human nature, shall we see and
understand ourselves and others.

HEROES OF HUMBLE LIFE

THE heroic death of Thomas Hovenden, who painted *The Last Hours of John Brown*, discloses to us the secret of his spiritual insight and keen appreciation of the majesty and glory of self-sacrifice. We wondered that the man who gave us *Breaking Home Ties* could understand so well the character of that stalwart old martyr whose deathless soul will go marching on as long as American history shall be remembered. It is all plain now. He was himself of the race of heroes, and what he has preserved to us of John Brown was substantially true of himself. The great Abolitionist, about to die upon the scaffold for a race of slaves, imprints a kiss upon the dusky forehead of a negro child in token of his love for the oppressed; and Thomas Hovenden, who fixed this scene upon canvas, gives his own beautiful life without a moment's hesitation, in the vain attempt to save that of a little girl who is to him an utter stranger. "Greater love," said our Lord, "hath no man than this,

that a man lay down his life for his friends,"—
these included in the noblest and most unsel-
fish love, the children of the lowly from whom
no material compensation could be expected;
and in that love there was something not of
this earth alone, but of that "Jerusalem the
Golden," of which Hovenden has given so
divine a vision upon canvas luminous with a
light more effulgent than that of mere genius.
The heroes are not all perished from off the
face of the earth. Amid the self-indulgence
and careless ease of a luxurious age are men
and women equal to any emergency, and not
one whit inferior to the saintly and courageous
souls of antiquity. It was the privilege of the
writer to know one such, not many years ago,
in a little village under the shadow of the
Berkshire hills. She was a New England
school-teacher, who crowned a life of thirty-
eight years, passed in the long monotony of
continuous self-sacrifice, with a death so heroic
that all the country where she lived cherishes
the remembrance of it with mingled reverence
and pride. She was a woman who knew well
the value of life, and took the keenest delight
in its rich treasures and even richer promises.
She had much to live for and to rejoice in,
even when her life was most conspicuous for
its self-renunciation. Yet when called to make

voluntary surrender of that life, under most painful circumstances, in an hour of appalling calamity, there was not even a moment of weakness or hesitancy. How little did the boys and girls in the village school, and the friends who knew her best, dream that day by day there abode with them, a sharer in their common joys and sorrows, one worthy the companionship of the most exalted heroes of chivalry and daring! The memorial library in Bryant Schoolhouse, under the spreading elms of Great Barrington, will preserve for many a year the name of Ida V. Roraback, making clear to the minds of youth and maiden the surpassing beauty and nobleness of a life sacred to duty, and of a death crowned with a love that casteth out fear. It is an inspiration to believe that in our homes, counting-houses, offices, and streets, in city and hamlet alike, are men and women to whom the greatest sacrifices and surrenders are forever possible. It cheers and encourages the heart in seasons of faintness and depression to remember that

" Such as these have lived and died."

By the side of the New England school-teacher may be placed a French Sister of Charity. The two are different enough, the one from the other, in all the externals of life and faith, yet they have a common part in the love and heroism that make all noble souls to be of one fellowship. Not long ago, in a city of France, all the soldiers were drawn up on the plaza. A woman in the habit of a Sister of Charity was called out in front of the Governor-General, and this is what he said:

"Mother Mary Teresa, when you were twenty years of age you received a wound from a cannon-ball while assisting one of the wounded on the field at Balaklava. In 1859 the shell from a mitrailleuse laid you prostrate in the front ranks on the battlefield of Magenta. Since then you have been in Syria, in China, and in Mexico, and if you were not wounded it was not because you have not exposed yourself.

"In 1870 you were taken up in Reischoffen covered with many sabre-wounds. Such deeds of heroism you crowned a few weeks ago with one of the most heroic actions which history records. A grenade fell upon the ambulance which was under your charge—you took up the grenade in your arms; you smiled upon the wounded who looked at you with feelings of dismay; you carried it a distance of eighty metres. On laying it down you noticed that it was going to burst; you threw yourself on the ground, it burst; you were seen covered with blood, but when persons came to your assistance you rose up smiling, as is your wont. You were scarcely recovered from your wound when you returned to the hospital whence I have now summoned you.''

Then the General made her kneel down, and, drawing his sword, touched her lightly with it three times on the shoulder, and pinned the Cross of the Legion of Honor on her habit, saying:

"I put upon you the cross of the brave, in the name of the French people and army. No one has gained it by more deeds of heroism, nor by a life so completely spent in self-abnegation for the benefit of your brothers and the service of your country. Soldiers, present arms!''

The troops saluted, the drums and bugles rang out, the air was filled with loud acclamations, and all was jubilation and excitement as Mother Teresa arose, her face suffused with blushes, and asked:

"General, are you done?''

"Yes,'' said he.

"Then I will go back to the hospital!''

It is not out of place here to record the deed of another hero whose name should be remembered and cherished:

"Speaking of the bubonic plague,'' said a New Orleans physician, "I doubt whether the entire

history of the world affords a more remarkable
example of personal heroism than was exhibited by
Dr. Franz Mueller of Vienna, who fell a victim to
the disease when it was first under bacteriological
investigation in that city, in 1897. Dr. Mueller
contracted the malady from the bacilli in ‘ culture
tubes,’ and when it became certain that he was
infected he immediately locked himself in an iso-
lated room and posted a message on the window
pane, reading thus:

“ ‘ I am suffering from plague. Please do not
send a doctor to me, as, in any event, my end will
come in four or five days.’

“A number of his associates were anxious to at-
tend him, but he refused to admit them and died
alone, within the time he predicted. He wrote a
farewell letter to his parents, placed it against the
window, so it could be copied from the outside,
and then burned the original with his own hands,
fearful it might be preserved and carry out the
mysterious germ. Mueller was a young man, on
the threshold of a brilliant scientific career, and
there was a chance that he might have been saved
by treatment, but he refused to take it, because it
entailed the risk of spreading the contagion
abroad.”

Apropos of heroism, it may be said that true
courage is essentially joyous. No doubt some
of the greatest and best of our race, from the
Man of Sorrows down to saintly ones of our

11

own time, have walked in gloom; yet their
courage had no part in casting the shadow,
and certainly did much to relieve the grievous
weight of its pressure. He who tasted death
for us all uttered in the darkness and anguish
of the supreme crisis of His most bitter passion
those remarkable words: "These things have
I spoken unto you, that My joy might remain in you, and that your joy might be full."
The inherent gladness of genuine courage,
whether physical or moral, is exhibited with
peculiar force in the literature of the ancient
Greeks, and may be viewed upon many a page
of Homer. Always the heroes turn them toward the sunrise. They delight in the unconventional freedom of the natural world, and
are at home under twinkling stars and swinging boughs. A large portion of the life of
Jesus was passed in the open air. I never
knew of a hero who disliked children, animals,
and flowers. Attention has been called to
three heroes: the Abolitionist comes down to
us on canvas, kissing, in the hour of his death,
a slave-child; the artist gives his life to preserve that of a little girl; and the school-
teacher devotes all her days to the boys and
girls of a New England village. In each life
is an echo of the beautiful and divine invitation:
"Suffer the little children, and forbid them

not to come unto Me." Children, animals, and
flowers are the natural symbols of gladness.
These are associated in our thoughts with ful-
ness of life and exuberance of feeling. They
are also the very embodiment of unconven-
tionality. King and peasant are equally ac-
ceptable to the democratic tastes of little
children. Left to themselves, children live
with the animals and flowers out-of-doors.
The beautiful palace was to the young prince
only a miserable prison, when, gazing down
from the window, he discovered the gardener's
son making mud-pies by the river-bank; and
his cry had in it a world of pathos: "Oh, the
beautiful mud!" A child is plundered of the
best treasures of childhood when separated
from the wholesome influences of nature, and
changed into a sickly product of the hothouse.
It may develop into a beau, a society lady, a
book-worm, or a money-maker, but it is surely
deprived of the material from which in later
years strong heart, steady nerves, steel sinews,
and an eye keen to pierce to the soul of things
are to be evolved. Far behind the calamity
that brings the heroic quality in a man's nature
to view is an unseen, silent, and yet continuous
growth of those elements within him that are
at last to bear the consummate flower and fruit
of nobleness. One such element is an inherent

cheerfulness of disposition.   There can be no
growth without warmth and light from the
sun.   Mental depression wears away self-confidence, and decreases the power of resistance
and the quality of resiliency.   Because the
jester Pellicanus, in Eber's *A Word, Only a
Word*, has learned to master and control a sadness that cannot be wholly crushed, and has
accustomed himself to season poverty and ill-
health with good-will and kindly merrymaking,
he has come into possession of a beautiful courage wherewith he faces his hard lot in manly
dignity and something of Christian patience.

" Sorrow," it is written in the *Tusculan Questions*,
" is repugnant to fortitude.   It is probable, then,
that whoever is subject to sorrow is also subject to
fear, and to a certain breaking down and dejection
of mind.   To the man for whom these are incident,
it is incident, also, to be mastered, and that he
should acknowledge himself at length overcome."

We would not affirm what the Latin writer
seems to declare,—that sorrow is, in and of
itself, unmanly and unproductive of good.
Christian ethics teach a different doctrine, for
there is a "godly sorrow that needeth not to
be repented of," and that ennobles the soul
that entertains it.   But of this we are sure,—
that habitual courage is fostered and increased

by habitual cheerfulness and a joyous disposition. The tap-root of true heroism is in neither intellect nor external circumstance, but in a human heart that has experienced the emancipating and uplifting power of that perfect love which, the sacred writer tells us, "casteth out fear."

No man can become a true hero who does not preserve within his bosom something of that beautiful faith in his fellow-men which gives freshness and enthusiasm to the dewy morning of life. The youth is plundered of all heroic inclinations and desires who permits the hard experiences and disillusionments of the world to destroy his respect for human nature. He who believes that "every man has his price" is most likely himself purchasable, and, perhaps, at no very high figure. The philosopher who called the world an ass was not much of a philosopher when he so unwittingly exposed his own large and pendulous ears; nor was he a hero, for how can one be a hero who is so meanly descended, and before whom stretches so hopeless a field for the display of manly valor? You will look in vain for a hero among habitual fault-finders and incorrigible money-lovers. A man told me it was his opinion that the world might be divided into two classes,—fools and knaves; yet,

strange to say, he was offended when I inquired of him to which of the two classes he
belonged.   We see the world through our own
eyes, and all life takes the color of our own
living.   Heroism begets heroism, and one
must himself believe in noble and courageous
men in order to be of their number.   Why
should he not believe in such?   Is that world
an ass, and so utterly base of nature, that can
give us the great patriots in history, and the
self-sacrificing and beloved mothers in all our
homes?\ Faith in the quality of goodness
underlies every possibility of heroism.   Without it no high ideal can be entertained.

But with all the optimism of his outlook and
all his faith in human nature, the man of heroic
mould is still a man of war.

" When the fight begins within himself,
   A man 's worth something.   God stoops o'er his
      head,
   Satan looks up between his feet—both tug—
   He 's left, himself, i' the middle; the soul wakes
   And grows.   Prolong that battle through his life!
   Never leave growing till the life to come! "

" Let a man contend to the uttermost
   For his life's set prize, be what it will! "

Let peace societies contemplate the fundamental, universal, and divine truth that it is

only "when the fight begins within himself,
a man 's worth something." The fight of
which the poet sings is no doubt entirely subjective, the man's moral nature being the
battlefield; still conflict that enriches the soul
enriches as well the life. There is nothing
good in unjust and unproductive strife, but
unless "a man contend to the uttermost," he
shall never have the prize. The presence of
evil is in itself a call to arms, and no man is
loyal to his nobler nature who fails of respond-
ing. It is in that fierce battle one must wage
with self and every base inclination that "the
soul wakes and grows;" and if so be he "prolong that battle through his life," he shall
"never leave growing till the life to come."
The old hymn so often sung in the church of
our childhood inquires:

> " Must I be carried to the skies
>   On flowery beds of ease,
>   While others fought to win the prize,
>   And sailed through bloody seas?"

A divine answer is returned in the language of
this same hymn, "I must fight if I would
reign"—an answer endorsed by the entire history of mankind as well as by human con-
sciousness itself, and emphasized by all nature

in that ceaseless strife through which countless creatures ever rise to higher planes.

What is true of the subjective is equally so of the objective life of man. "By their fruits ye shall know them"—from what a man does we know what he is; and, conversely, what a man is will determine his conduct. He cannot contend against evil within himself and yet make no opposition to evil in the world around him. If the fight within be sincere, the battle in his life will amount to more than protest— it will come to open and decided action. When the "soul wakes and grows," the exterior and visible life also "wakes and grows."

Whatever is true of the individual is likewise true of the nation, which is but a collection of individuals acting in concert. Much may be accomplished by means of arbitration and the advance of Christian civilization, yet it will remain true that growth implies some degree of strife and ferment.

Ruskin's opinion of war, in his *Crown of Wild Olive*, may appear to the peace societies a savage voice out of a wild and turbulent past, but its foundations rest upon an unassailable truth:

"When I tell you that war is the foundation of all the arts I mean also that it is the foundation of all the high virtues and faculties of men. It was very strange to me to discover this, and very dreadful, but I saw it to be quite an undeniable fact. . . . I found, in brief, that all great nations learnt their truth of word and strength of thought in war, that they were nourished in war and wasted by peace, taught by war and deceived by peace, trained by war and betrayed by peace, in a word, that they were born in war and expired in peace."

With fine ethical discrimination, Dr. Martineau writes:

" The reverence for human life is carried to an immoral idolatry when it is held more sacred than justice and right, and when the spectacle of blood becomes more horrible than the sight of desolating tyrannies and triumphant hypocrisies. . . . A religion which does not include the whole moral law; a moral law which does not embrace all the problems of a commonwealth; a commonwealth which regards the life of man more than the equities of God, appear to be unfaithful to their functions, and unworthy interpreters of the divine scheme of the world."

ART AND LIFE

THE difficulty with modern art, especially such art as we create and understand in this Western world, is its separation from life. It is a thing apart by itself, to which we repair at times for purposes in no wise ideal. Art is one thing and life another. The former has lost its vitality, and, as a natural consequence, the latter has parted from its reverence and aspiration. The self-sufficiency of each is responsible for the dull-eyed selfishness of both. With us the arts do not

> " receive
> The natural man;
> And educate him, step by step,
> Unto the master-art—
> The art of Life."

Poetry is, at least in external and visible expression, an art. Mr. Austin, the English Laureate, defines it as "the transfiguration of the actual or the real into the ideal." Un-transfigured, the common, every-day world that seems to all of us so real, is dull and prosaic. It loses all its spiritual significance. In his Address before the Royal Institution, Mr. Austin uttered these suggestive words: "Men and women of a former generation seized with eager hands on a new poem, read it with fervent tenderness, returned to it again and again, learned much of it by heart, and gave it a permanent place in their thoughts and affections." That is so no longer, and never again can it be so unless we return to the old cement of religious thinking and feeling. The union of art and life is essentially spiritual. Emerson tells us that "the Gothic cathedrals were built when the builder and the priest and the people were overpowered by their faith." The highest art, though by no means necessarily Christian, is always religious. Its nature is religious, and its purpose devotional. It gives rise to a sense of worship. Thus it came to pass that the cathedrals, the great pictures, and the best music grew up in ages of faith, and themselves inspired faith wherever they prevailed. Only with the return of deep religious conviction and feeling can art and life, now unfortunately separated, be once more united. The religious element is that of unification. Push back far enough in the history of our race and you shall see that it once dominated the entire life of man. In the time of such domination all human experience was a unit. We hear much of "art for art's sake," but nothing truly great exists for itself alone. The art that looks no higher than its own expression is not art, for it lacks the transforming spirit of love; and without that spirit "the transfiguration of the actual" is impossible. In the very word *religio*, which means, "again I bind," is contained this great truth.

WHAT SHALL WE BELIEVE?

IT is difficult to say what is to be believed in these days of original investigation and measureless denial. Many a year has gone by since the witty German, Lichtenberg, said:

" Our world will grow so refined that it will be just as ridiculous to believe in God as nowadays in ghosts. And then after a while the world will grow more refined still. And so it will go on with the greatest rapidity to the utmost summit of refinement. Having attained the pinnacle, the judgment of the wise will be reversed; knowledge will change itself for the last time. Then—and this will be the end—then shall we believe in nothing-ghosts."

Lichtenberg's prediction has come true, only this is not the end.

There appears to be still another stage in the delectable process of refinement. From believing in "nothing-ghosts," we are coming to question even these; and some of us are already so wise that we doubt doubt. The dying confession of John Theophilus Fichte may become the gospel of the next century:

"I know absolutely nothing of any existence, not even of my own. Images there are, and they constitute all that apparently exists. I am myself one of those images; nay, not so much, but only a confused image of an image. All reality is converted into a marvellous dream, without a life to dream of, or a mind to dream; into a dream itself made up only of a dream. Perception is a dream; and thought, the source of all the existence, the reality of which I imagine to myself, is but the dream of that dream."

Extremes meet. I inquired of a darkey what was his religious belief, and was surprised to see him square off like a prize-fighter, as he replied: "Boss, I 's a philosopher, an' don' belieb nuffing any more." At last the wise German and the, to my mind, equally wise darkey shake hands. For them both the poet has prepared a musical and drowsy motto that would have delighted Diodorus, surnamed Chronos the Slow, who wrote a treatise on the "Awful Nothing" and died in despair:

"Thinking is but idle waste of thought,
  And naught is everything, and everything is naught."

John Locke, David Hume, John Stuart Mill,
and Herbert Spencer are come, spade in hand,
to dig the grave of the human soul.   But since
they find it impossible to agree among themselves just where and how deep the grave shall
be, the soul need be in no haste about dying.
It seems clear enough from the philosophical
altercations of these distinguished gentlemen
that the funeral must be indefinitely postponed.

Very entertaining are the genial and gifted
English materialistic philosophers, who define
matter in the terms of spirit, and spirit in the
terms of matter; and so go round and round
the caldron in a ceaseless witch-dance.   They
seem to have become self-intoxicated through
the whirling motion of their own speculative
activity.   In the end—if there be anything like
an end to a circle—their entire system comes
to *vox et præterea nihil*.   The poet puts it into
five lines:

> " For the upshot of all preaching is :
>   What a man has done
>   Is the thing he does.
> And the upshot of all teaching is :
>   Man can be taught but what he knows."

Froude, in his rectorial address at St. Andrews, and Kingsley, in a lecture at Cambridge,
came to rhetorical and dialectical blows, each

declaring that he had no confidence in the other's branch of learning.   Out of this literary set-to came the witty epigram:

> " Froude informs the Scottish youth
> That parsons have no care for truth ;
> While Canon Kingsley loudly cries
> That history is a pack of lies.
> What cause for judgment so malign ?
> A brief reflection solves the mystery ;
> For Froude thinks Kingsley a divine,
> And Kingsley goes to Froude for history."

Well, it is certainly difficult to say what one is to believe, not only in theology and history, but in nearly every department of human learning. Long ago I surrendered the story of Pocahontas and Captain John Smith, and the beautiful myth of William Tell and the apple, and now—*O tempora! O mores!*—George Washington and his little hatchet must be deliberately sacrificed to the nescience of this unbelieving century.

It seems to be the universal opinion that George did have a hatchet, and yet the "higher critics" are sure to a man that the youngster told more lies in a brief quarter of an hour than there were cherries on the famous tree he did not cut down.   And Lucrezia Borgia—blessed be the pious memory of that angelic woman!

—the "riper scholarship" (a Philistine leaning over my shoulder wants me to substitute "rotten" for "riper") of this age has discovered that she was, after all the scandal, little less than one of the most beautiful of saints. There is an absurd story that the last words of Daniel Webster were, "I still live"; but even Appela, the superstitious Jew, knows that the last words of the illustrious Daniel were, "Weep not for me, kind friends, for I am by no means a fresh corpse; I have been politically dead these many years." When I was a boy they believed—simple-hearted creatures!—that Cambronne said at the battle of Waterloo, "The guards die, but they never surrender." Schoolmaster Schram beat that into my head by way of the *flexor profundus digitorum* with a brass-bound hickory ruler, and now it appears that the great man said nothing of the kind—what he did say is this: "The guards surrender every time, and usually die of old age." Suspense is torture. Let us have done with everything at once. I make the crowning concession, and, with the immortal Ignatius Donnelly, turn over the less immortal plays of Shakespeare to the mighty shade of Bacon.

DR. TUCKER'S LAST REQUEST

" The exceeding thoughtfulness of the late Rev. Dr. J. Ireland Tucker, the beloved rector of the Church of the Holy Cross, was shown in connection with the selection of his burial plat in Oakwood. Dr. Tucker said that there would be many children and aged people who would desire to visit his grave, and so it would be best that a lot be secured near the entrance, that they might be saved the trouble of walking far. However, before Dr. Tucker's death it was found that a suitable lot could not be obtained in the desired location. A plat in the new part of the cemetery seemed to be the best that could be purchased, but Dr. Tucker was so intent on having a lot as at first intended that the arrangements for the purchase were not completed until after his death.

" Dr. Tucker's remains were placed in the centre of the plat, and, as the dead rector requested, 'where the sun will shine on them all the day.' In accordance with Dr. Tucker's wishes, any of the poor of the church who so desire may be buried in the remainder of the ground."

THIS touching and lovely record of thoughtful affection, taken from the Troy *Times* of August 22, 1895, reminds us of the gentle Minnesinger who, from the darkness of the thirteenth century, sings to us and to all mankind like the birds that nested in his gracious name and banqueted above his tomb. We forget the defeated Heinrich von Ofterdingen and the musical war of Wartburg when we think of those four holes in the stone that covered his dust, from which the heavenly choir of "feathered minnesingers" gathered the daily store of yellow corn. The spirit of the good rector of Holy Cross had in it something akin to that of the brave and kindly man who was not so great a poet, even while his voice was heard through all the German land, that he could not feel the tie that bound him firmly, yet gently, to all animate creatures. Perhaps Walther von der Vogelweide remembered the pious bishop at Zeisselmauer on the Danube, whose gold bought him the fur coat that kept him warm in the frosty air of northern winters. Perhaps his thoughts were of the stout-hearted peasants in their wooden shoes, who followed his lead against pope and oppressor. Perhaps he was considering only how much he had learned of wandering life and free-hearted song from the gay minstrels of the

air. Whatever was in his mind, his bequest
to the birds was an acknowledgment of no small
obligation, but of a debt paid to all when paid
to the humblest of God's creatures. "Bury
me where the sun will shine upon my grave
all the day, and let the poor who will share in
my resting-place,"—these words are but our
English way of saying what was in the German heart of the old Minnesinger: "Let me
repose where a leafy tree shall cast its shadow,
and the light of the summer day shall linger
long; and feed my brother singers of the air
from the stone above my tomb."

THE *PÈRE LA CHAISE* OF AMERICA

WITH peculiar propriety Mount Auburn Cemetery in Cambridge, Mass., is called the *Père La Chaise* of America. Within its sacred inclosures repose, surrounded by the combined loveliness of nature and art, some of the most gifted of our race,—sons and daughters of deathless song, children of the arts, heroes of the noblest achievements, eloquent apostles of Heaven's gospel of peace, rare scholars, and philanthropists whose lives were beautiful with compassion and fragrant with self-sacrifice. There, "'neath solitudes of shade and many a canopy of green," great names are carved in marble and cast in bronze: Johann Kaspar Spurzheim, born far away in a little village near the city of Treves on the Moselle; John Pierpont, the preacher-poet who wrote the devout and graceful hymn sung when Mount Auburn was consecrated; John Murray and William Ellery Channing, names ever dear to Universalists and Unitarians; Henry Wadsworth Longfellow and James Russell Lowell, poets of the most tender and beautiful sentiments—rich in scholarship and lovers of freedom; Oliver Wendell Holmes, whose wit and kindly genius unlocked all hearts; Nathaniel Parker Willis, the most elegant and fastidious of all our American men of letters; William Hickling Prescott, whose *Ferdinand and Isabella, Conquest of Mexico,* and *Philip the Second* are among the most brilliant and superbly scenic of historical works; John Lothrop Motley, the man of world-wide culture, the far-seeing diplomat, the uncompromising patriot, and the conscientious historian ; Phillips Brooks, the good bishop whose helpful influence extended beyond his own sect, and made all the world his parish; Charles Sumner, one of the purest as well as one of the best-equipped of statesmen; Edwin Booth and Charlotte Saunders Cushman, than whom the world has seen few greater actors; and Louis Jean Rodolph Agassiz, the Swiss naturalist who loved America even better than the land of his nativity,—all these and many more whose names are imperishable rest amid the reverential solitudes of "the Field of Peace."

But there are other sepulchres in the beautiful garden cemetery of Mount Auburn than those wherein slumber the illustrious dead of

whom we so often read and think,—sepulchres
of the lowly and undistinguished, which are yet
of such peculiar interest that we cannot allow
them to sink into utter oblivion. Among these
may be mentioned the Strangers' Tomb, built
in 1833 by the proprietors of the Tremont
House in Boston, for the burial of strangers
dying at that hotel. It is a pentagonal vault,
containing thirty-six cells, radiating from the
common centre. Each cell is intended for the
reception of a single casket. Over the entire
vault is a pentagonal structure of Quincy
granite, about six feet high, and there in stillness and shadow repose two strangers,—Sidney
Hayes of Smyrna, who died October 20, 1832,
and Jasper Macomb of New York, a United
States army officer, who died December 15,
1833. Tremont House has disappeared from
among the hotels of Boston, but Strangers'
Tomb on Hawthorne Path will continue an
abiding memorial of a generous and unmerce-
nary spirit.

Who remembers Warren Colburn? Yonder
is a freestone column sustaining an urn, and
in the stone is preserved that man's worthy
name. He was in his day a distinguished
mathematician, whose works on arithmetic and
algebra were in well-nigh every American, and
in many European schools. Where now are

his books, once the delight of eager publishers and the vexation of dull schoolboys? Gone, every one of them, to the shades of silence and oblivion. What a lesson to the living is that neglected tomb on Locust Avenue, slowly gathering to itself the dust and moss of long years!

The grave of Professor Webster is in Mount Auburn. Few remember the tragedy of half a century ago, and now but little interest attaches to the grassy mound and weather-beaten monument that mark the resting-place of a once distinguished man, whose life went out in the darkness of a great crime.

On Central Avenue is a white marble shaft inscribed with the name of Hannah Adams. Our fathers read her *History of the Jews* and her *Reviews of the Christian Sects*, but who knows anything about that woman and her books now? Her name may be found in a few biographical dictionaries, and upon the stone raised to her memory in Mount Auburn, and beyond these there remains to this generation nothing of Hannah Adams.

Time was when the boys of the Boston Latin School knew well the gifted and honored Frederic P. Leverett, and some of us still value his *Latin Lexicon*, the last page of which went to press the very day of his death. On Vine Path the literary pilgrim may behold the quiet rest-ing-place where, sixty years ago, the industrious and elegant classicist found that dreamless re-pose from which the circling ages shall not arouse him.

THE MODERN VIEW OF DEATH

A N enlightened Christian civilization has greatly modified the popular conception of death. Men long held in bondage to the fear of the grave are escaping from the dungeon. Skeletons and cross-bones are giving place to heavenly angels, emblems of Christian faith, and wreaths of victory. The old pagan gloom and despair are melting like snow in the warm rays of a living gospel. Memorial Day is an illustration. It began with two or three broken-hearted women strewing flowers on the graves of men dear to them, who had fought with valor in the Confederate army. Northern women saw the beauty and felt the propriety of such an offering, and followed the example of their sisters in the South. Our fathers spoke of death as the king of terrors, but we contemplate man's dissolution in quite a different light. Death is a reaper gathering precious grain, "and the flowers that grow between," for the heavenly garner. The rabbis taught that there

were three drops of gall on the sword of death:
one enters the mouth and the man dies; the
second suffuses the face with pallor; and the
third turns the flesh into dust. But for all
who consider mortality in the light of Christian
faith, the sword is forever sheathed, and death
is swallowed up in victory. An old-time author
wrote centuries ago these quaint words:

" Death is but a dormitory for a day.—The
Grave is but a with-drawing roome to retire in for
a while, a going to bed to take rest sweeter than
sleepe.—In the Grave all looke alike, *Lazarus*
sores will make as good dust as *Jezebels* paint.—
The graine cast into the earth, after a frost-biting,
comes up the fairer.—Man is only a wink of life,
his life and death joyned as neere as joy and
griefe; where teares (the limbecke of the Heart)
expresse both.—The labourer from his worke hastens to his bed; The Mariner rowes hard to gaine
the Port, The Traveller is glad when he is within
kenning of his Inne; yet wee, when death comes to
put us into our port, shun it as a Rocke.—Some
will dye for wantonnesse, if they want their wils.
. . . Every one is here set Centinel, and not
to leave the place till his Captaine call him off."

THE CAMPO SANTO OF THE DIS-
SENTERS

ADDISON, who was no melancholy senti-
mentalist, wrote:

"When I look upon the tombs of the great,
every emotion of envy dies within me; when I read
the epitaphs of the beautiful, every inordinate desire
goes out; when I meet with the grief of parents
upon a tombstone, my heart melts with compassion; when I see the tombs of the parents themselves, I consider the vanity of grieving for those
whom we must quickly follow. When I see kings
lying by those who deposed them, when I consider
rival wits side by side, or the holy men that divided
the world with their contests and disputes, I reflect
with sorrow and astonishment on the little com-
petitions, factions, and debates of mankind. When
I read the several dates on the tombs of some that
died yesterday, and some six hundred years ago,
I consider that great day when we shall all of
us be contemporaries, and make one appearance
together."

Dull indeed must be the mind that can draw
no useful lesson from the solemn stillness of
Santa Croce, Saint Onofrio, Mount Vernon,
and that most sacred of all places, the Holy
Sepulchre. Who that cares for history and
delights in art can view unmoved the beautiful sarcophagus of Scipio, the feudal crypt of
Theodoric, the mossy pyramid of Caius Cæstus,
Thorwaldsen's wonderful mausoleum at Copen-
hagen, or the glorious resting-place of the
"silent soldier of the Invalides?" What immortal voices call from lonely catacombs and
rock-hewn caves by the deserted Nile! What
devout courage, inspiration, and gratitude well
up in the heart of the Christian pilgrim to
holy shrines, as with deeply religious awe he
presses the green turf of Bunhill Fields Burial
Ground, and in that great "Campo Santo of
the Dissenters" pauses to view the spot where
John Bunyan awaits the dawning of that day
for which all other days were made!

It was a faultless April afternoon when the
writer passed through the little inner gate half
covered with rust that shuts out from the
wild-rushing current of London life the quiet
repose of Bunhill Fields Burial Ground, and
stood by the tomb of the great dreamer whose
divine allegory will live until the last pilgrim
from the City of Destruction shall have entered

into the rest which remaineth for the people of God. The monument is hardly in accord with the heavenly simplicity of character which distinguished the man whose memory it enshrines. It is a high altar-tomb, supporting a life-size recumbent statue of Bunyan, and chronicling the dates of his birth and death. Its modern construction (it was erected in the year 1862) is a standing reproach to the English people, and a striking commentary upon the ingratitude of posterity. For a hundred and seventy-eight years the rank grass waved uncut, and the wild flowers bloomed and faded ungathered, over the undistinguished dust of that wonderful man, whose *Pilgrim's Progress* Coleridge has called "the best *Summa Theologiæ Evangelica* ever produced by a writer not miraculously inspired."

The tomb of Bunyan is surrounded by the hallowed graves of more than three hundred Nonconformist ministers, most of whom were ejected from their churches for no other crime than that of obedience to enlightened conscience and the exercise of manly courage. They were men of splendid proportion; dauntless in spirit as they were spotless in life; and wherever English language and history shall be known, the calm and religious trust with which they endured the hatred of their foes, and the courage with which they took the spoiling of their goods, must excite the warmest admiration.   They loved, as only heroic souls can love, the grand old prisoner of Bedford jail, and it was the last request of many of them: "Bury me in the Bonehill Fields, and let my coffin be as near as possible to that of the author of *Pilgrim's Progress.*"   There they all rest to-day in what was once derisively called "the fanatical burial-place," and over well-nigh every grave might be written the beautiful word PEACE.   " They shall hunger no more, neither thirst any more; neither shall the sun light on them, nor any heat."   The trial of their faith is ended, and " the fanatical burial-place" is consecrated ground indeed.

We notice the altar tomb of Richard Cromwell, looking old and somewhat neglected; and not far away is the grave of the devout Dr. Thomas Goodwin, who prayed with the dying Oliver Cromwell, and invoked the blessing of Heaven upon his son Richard when he was proclaimed Protector.   Meagre was the blessing that came in response to that prayer, for the "Merry Monarch" soon ruled in the place of the weak and irresolute Richard.   We linger a few moments by the quiet resting-place of one of the wisest and best of men, the great Dr. Nathaniel Lardner, whose *Credibility of Gospel History* has made the entire Christian world debtor to his consecrated scholarship. Yonder is the tomb of Thomas Bradbury, who scorned the bribe of a bishopric; the grave of Hansard Knollys, whose *Flaming Fire in Zion* made him renowned; the grave of Daniel Neal, who wrote *The History of the Puritans;* the grave of Theophilus Gale, who was the author of the *Court of the Gentiles,* and was turned out from his fellowship at Magdalen because, refusing obedience to priestly rule, he chose "rather to suffer affliction with the people of God;" the grave of Vavasour Powell, called "the Whitefield of Wales,"— the man who hated monarchy and episcopacy with a perfect hatred, and who was willing to remain in the Fleet Prison eleven years and to die there for "a Church without a Bishop, and a State without a King."

In the midst of this "glorious company" and "goodly fellowship" rises the monument of Bunyan. The author of *The Pilgrim's Progress* was not a whit behind his brethren in willingness to suffer for conscience' sake. Twelve and a half long years he was shut up in Bedford jail. Upon another occasion he was imprisoned six months. Shut out from the society of his fellow-men, he gave himself up to the study of the Bible and the *Book of*

Martyrs, and employed his time in preaching to and praying with his fellow-prisoners, and in working at laces for his own support and that of his family until it pleased God to bring him forth into open day, to give the world for all time to come a book worthy of the place to which Macaulay assigns it, by the side of *Paradise Lost*.

A few steps from the tomb of Bunyan, and we are at the grave of a holy woman, whose memory will always be reverently cherished by Methodists, because she was the mother of John Wesley. A simple headstone marks her resting-place, and upon it the pilgrim may read this epitaph:

" HERE

LIES THE BODY OF SUSANNAH WESLEY,

WIDOW OF THE REV'D SAMUEL WESLEY, M. A.,

LATE RECTOR OF EPWORTH

IN

LINCOLNSHIRE,

WHO DIED JULY 23, 1712, AGED 73 YEARS.

" She was the youngest daughter of Rev. Samuel Annesley, D.D., ejected by the act of uniformity from the Rectory of St. Giles, Cripplegate, August 24, 1662. She was the mother of nineteen children,

13

of whom the most eminent were Revs. John and
Charles Wesley, the former of whom was, under
God, the founder of the Societies of People called
Methodists.

" In sure and steadfast hope to rise
And claim her mansions in the skies,
A Christian here her flesh laid down,
The cross exchanging for a crown.

" True daughter of affliction she,
Inured to pain and misery,
Mourn'd a long night of griefs and fears,
A legal night of seventy years.

" The Father then reveal'd His Son,
Him in the broken bread made known,
She knew and felt her sins forgiven,
And found the earnest of her Heaven.

" Meet for the fellowship above,
She heard the cry, 'Arise, my Love!'
' I come,' her dying looks replied,
And lamb-like as her Lord she died."

The words, "Him in the broken bread made
known," set forth her firm belief that it was at
the Lord's Supper, while receiving from her
son-in-law the sacred elements, she obtained
assurance that her sins were forgiven.   Her

last request discloses her character, and shows how strong was her faith: "Children," she said, "so soon as I am released, sing a psalm of praise to God." Accordingly, when she had ceased breathing, her children, who were gathered round the bed, sang with confident voices, but not without tears of sorrow, a song of praise. Her son John conducted the funeral service, and preached a sermon from the words of Scripture: "I saw the dead, small and great, stand before God; and the books were opened; and another book was opened, which is the book of life: and the dead were judged out of those things which were written in the books, according to their works." Impressive, indeed, must have been the sight of that vast congregation gathered among the tombs to hear John Wesley, over his mother's grave, warn men of the uncertainty of life and of the nearness of death and judgment. Wesley himself has left us this record: "It was one of the most solemn assemblies I ever saw, or expect to see, on this side eternity."

Not far away from the resting-place of the mother of the Wesleys is the tomb of Dr. John Owen, a pious, learned, and courageous author and preacher, whose sermons and books exerted great influence over the seventeenth-century thought of England. Dr. Owen, though for a time connected with the Presbyterians, was at heart an Independent, and sympathized with Congregationalism; and when opportunity presented itself he established and ministered to a church of that order. His scholarship won for him so enviable a reputation, not only in his own country but beyond the sea, that in 1663 the Congregational churches of Boston, in New England, invited him to settle with them. He declined the call, and a few years later criticised with just severity a spirit of persecution and of theological bitterness which had appeared in Massachusetts, and was endangering the fair fame of its churches. The rebuke does not seem to have rendered him unpopular upon this side of the Atlantic, for in 1670 Harvard University elected him to its presidency, and at one time it was thought he would accept what was even at that early day a great honor. As a Nonconformist preacher and writer Dr. Owen often plunged into violent disputes, and many were the deadly blows to Episcopacy and Romanism which emanated from his mighty brain. And now that brain, so wise and fertile in its day, is all dissolved in dust, and the pilgrim to Bunhill Fields may gather, as did the writer, on a bright April morning, English ivy-leaves, where one of the greatest of Dissenters awaits the coming of the only King before whose sovereignty he bowed with unquestioning submission.

Crossing the gravel-covered path that divides the burial-ground, we came upon the tomb of dear old Dr. Watts, who in 1748, having filled the Church on earth with sacred song, went himself to join the holier song of the redeemed in heaven. Around the large altar-tomb of this famous Independent minister and saintly hymn-writer some friendly hand arranges every year a little bed of flowers. Kneeling in the long grass to pluck a bud for memory's sake, and calling to mind the strong and noble life of that "singing Pilgrim" and "Soldier of the Cross," there came to the writer's heart and so to his lips the solemn and beautiful hymn he used to sing when a boy in the village church to which his father ministered:

> " Am I a soldier of the cross,
>   A follower of the Lamb?
>   And shall I fear to own His cause,
>   Or blush to speak His name? "

Had Isaac Watts written nothing else, I could love his memory for the hymn of which that stanza is the opening one, and I confess that a spirit of hot indignation rises in my bosom when I read how its author, against whose character or faith no man can bring just

accusation, was insultingly called "a shorn
hypocrite" and "a psalm-singing bigot." The
simple truth is that the character of Watts was
one of peculiar beauty, and that his life was
marked by exceptional piety. Even Dr. John-
son, who was a strong "Churchman," speaking
of Watts, has felt himself constrained to put
on record this testimony: "Happy will be that
reader whose mind is disposed by his verse, or
his prose, to imitate him in all but his non-
conformity, to copy his benevolence to man
and his reverence to God."

In this "Campo Santo of the Dissenters,"
as Southey is pleased to call the old Puritan
burial-place, are the tombs of Joseph Hughes,
who founded the Bible Society; David Nas-
mith, to whom we owe City Missions; Joseph
Ritson, the antiquary; and William Blake, the
mad poet, painter, and engraver whose business
it was "not to gather gold, but to make glorious shapes, expressing godlike sentiments,"
and whose illustrations of the Book of Job,
Young's *Night Thoughts*, and Blair's *Grave*
are among the wonderful achievements of
art.

On the northern side of this little city of
tombs, near the grave of Watts, is a monument builded by the boys and girls of England,
over the dust of the butcher's son, Daniel

Defoe, whose *Robinson Crusoe* has thrilled the
hearts of children all over the world. The
early life of Defoe shows us how important are
right influences in moulding the disposition and
character of a boy, and his later years disclose
with striking force the truth of the old adage,
"The boy is father of the man." Daniel was
brought up at the famous dissenting academy
of Mr. Morton at Stoke Newington, where his
associations were of a most robust, pure, and
wholesome nature; and where he was taught
to have convictions, and to avow and defend
them. His schoolmates were, most of them,
children of nonconforming ministers, and were
destined, like himself, to play important parts
in the religious and political history of the
times. His great gift to the children of his
own and succeeding ages grew from seeds
planted in his youthful heart and nourished
by the bracing atmosphere of a stalwart Pro-
testantism; and the boys and girls of this and
other countries are as certainly indebted to the
principles of dissent for *Robinson Crusoe* as
are their parents to those same principles for
the greater work of *Pilgrim's Progress.* Daniel
Defoe's life was not an easy one. Misfortune
and persecution attended him, and the boldness
of his pen created for him many and powerful
enemies who ceased not to follow his memory

with hatred long after his body had crumbled into dust. Indeed the only authentic description of his personal appearance we possess comes from an offer of reward for his arrest, published by his foes. The description is reasonably minute, and sets him before us as "a middle-sized spare man about forty years old, of a brown complexion and dark brown coloured hair, but wears a wig; a hooked nose, a sharp chin, grey eyes, and a large mole near his mouth." The fame of *Robinson Crusoe* so overshadows all his other works that few think of him as the gifted author of *Moll Flanders*, *The Journal of the Plague* (now called, from the title of the second edition, *A History of the Plague*), and *The Shortest Way with Dissenters*. The last-named book was written from a "Churchman's" standpoint and occasioned the wildest excitement among all classes of religionists. It revealed with startling candor the actual feeling entertained by English ecclesiastics toward their dissenting brethren, and exposed to view the monstrous conclusions to which Prelacy must inevitably conduct its disciples.

Near the centre of Bunhill Fields Burial Ground is the quaint tomb of Dame Mary Page with this curious inscription upon its face:

HERE LYES DAME MARY PAGE,
RELICT OF SIR GREGORY PAGE, BAR'T.
SHE DEPARTED THIS LIFE MARCH 11, 1728,
IN THE 56 YEAR OF HER AGE.
IN 67 MONTHS SHE WAS TAP'D 66 TIMES,
HAD TAKEN AWAY 240 GALLONS OF WATER,
WITHOUT EVER REPINEING AT HER CASE
OR EVER FEARING THE OPERATION.

Dame Mary Page, it seems, belonged as truly to the race of heroes as did the great Nonconformist ministers and writers whose dust mingles with hers in the great "Campo Santo of the Dissenters." It may be that she glorified God quite as much by her patient submission to His will as did Bunyan and Powell by their adherence to truth under long imprisonment. All God requires of any of His children is faithful discharge of duty in the place to which He assigns the obedient soul. It is not necessary to do some great thing in order to secure the Divine blessing and the approval of conscience. "Do to-day thy nearest duty," whether it be pleasant or otherwise, and thou shalt well answer the end of life.

It has been truly said: "He was a witty man that first taught a stone to speak; but he was a wicked man that taught it first to lie." It adds greatly to the pleasure of a visit to Bunhill Fields to know that its ancient stones and

modern monuments tell few lies; and that the
men and women who slumber there rest in
peace awaiting the resurrection of the just.

" ' The Fathers are in dust, yet live to God,'
  So says the Truth; as if the motionless clay
  Still held the seeds of life beneath the sod,
  Smouldering and struggling till the judgment
    day.
  Sophist may urge his cunning test, and deem
  That they are earth; but they are heavenly
    shrines."

The lengthening and deepening shadows falling over the silent graves warned the pilgrim
of approaching night, and with reluctant feet
he sought the little iron gate, and turning its
rusty hinges found himself once more borne
onward like a fallen leaf by the tumultuous
current of London life.

DUST TO DUST

"DUST thou art and to dust shalt thou return" is written not of man only, but of all his works. We learn from Herodotus that the remains of Cheops were deposited between two colossal mounds of precious metal. Where are they—both dust and gold—to-day? In the British Museum the visitor may see a thin, withered, dry mummy, all smeared with bitumen and various resins. That mummy, it is believed, was Cleopatra, the beautiful and licentious queen whose palace on the Nile was filled with the wealth of many nations. Where are her palaces, her treasures, and her beauty? Gone forever. The earth can no longer give her a grave, and there under a glass case she lies, a curiosity in a museum. In the newly discovered mummies of Rameses II. (the great Sesostris and the Pharaoh in whose palace Moses lived for forty years) and of Rameses III., royal dust that once swayed the rod of empire over one of the mightiest kingdoms upon the face of the earth becomes the dishonored object of idle speculation and a source of amusement to the vulgar and profane. The celebrated Portland or Barberini vase, found in the sixteenth century in the marble sarcophagus of the Roman Emperor, Alexander Severus, was most likely that monarch's last resting-place, but now it is only a costly (Wedgwood valued it in 1786 at five thousand pounds) and beautiful ornament, from which artists shape forms of exquisite grace for homes of wealth and for great museums all over the civilized world. Who, visiting that wonderful treasure, gives one poor thought to the once powerful Emperor who centuries ago claimed it for his tomb? A great queen was placed in a coffin made of silver coins fastened together and valued at thirty thousand dollars. Much good it did her when the worm fed sweetly upon her damask cheek and grave-mould gathered over her silent lips! The crumbling ruins of the once magnificent Aztec empire breathe forth, as from the trembling strings of some vast Æolian harp stirred by the melancholy winds of destiny, the hopeless refrain of the Hebrew king, "Vanity of vanities, all is vanity." The grave of the ill-fated Montezuma is lost from the memory of man and his house is left desolate.

When we behold these things and allow them to influence our thoughts and feelings, how

true seem the words carved over the main
aisle of the cathedral at Milan: ".That only is
important which is eternal." How foolish in
the light of our common origin and destiny
appear the little distinctions of life; and how
unworthy of human nature seems that inordinate pride of ancestry which so often blinds its
possessor to the just claims of those who have
the misfortune to be sprung from humbler
sources! The unclean coprolite detracts nothing from the beauty of the polished beetle-
stone. That man is noble who " nobly lives
and does." He whom we call the perfected
flower of our race, and within whose divine
arms we are lifted up into communion with
God, entered this world by a stable door, and
departed out of it upon a cross.

The common fact of death should teach us
all a common charity. We too often forget
the good men have done in the over-contem-
plation of some flagrant fault or fatal crime
into which they have been betrayed by the
sudden temptation of an unguarded hour.
We deal unjustly with human nature when we
allow the shadow of an evil moment to darken
the otherwise luminous expanse of an entire
life. We are none of us so wicked as our
neighbors think us, nor yet so good as we
often fancy ourselves to be; and we should

ever remember that the most degraded of
mankind is still a sharer with us in a common
humanity. Benedict Arnold was a true hero
when, October 7, 1777, at Saratoga, he rode
his famous black horse, and led his soldiers
on to righteous victory. His later treachery
and infamy can never blot from history the
page that records his noble valor. It is true
that " the evil men do lives after them," and it
is unfortunately even more true that "the good
is often interred with their bones," but it is
not thus that God judges of His children, and
when we so judge we are not Godlike.

DEATH—AND AFTERWARDS

THERE was a world of human feeling in the bosom of Sir Nicholas Crispe. Having lived the life of a wealthy and influential citizen in old London, from which city he was driven in his last days by the vigilance of the House of Commons, he died and left a sum of money, the interest of which was to be used in refreshing his heart once in every year with a glass of the best wine that could be procured. For nearly a century the heart was annually taken from the urn and bathed in wine, until at last, through the frequent ablutions, it became so decayed that the ceremony had to be discontinued. Mr. Bancroft, who lived a long time ago in the same city, had very much the same feeling with regard to the after-death condition and wants of his body. He requested in his will that, for a century every year on the anniversary of his death, one loaf of bread and a bottle of wine should be deposited in the vault that contained his mortal frame. The bread and wine were to be placed

where he could reach them, and the coffin-lid
was to be lifted so that he could extend his
arm and lay hold of the provisions. There
was a man in Normandy in the early part of
the century who desired to be buried at night
in his bed, comfortably tucked in, with pillows
and coverlets as he had died. A huge pit was
sunk, and the corpse was lowered into its last
resting-place, without any alteration having
been made in the position in which death had
overtaken him. Boards were laid over the bed
so that the falling earth should not disturb
him. Mrs. George S. Norton, of Pawling, N.
Y., was buried at her own request sitting upright in a rocking-chair, enclosed in a box
made of seasoned chestnut.[1] Brigham Young,
it is said, wanted his coffin made large enough
to permit of his turning from one side to the
other.

Somehow we all want our hearts refreshed in
one way or another when we have joined the
great majority, and have no more part in the
activities of human life. We may not covet
Sir Nicholas Crispe's wine-bath; and it is more
than likely that bread and wine with an open
coffin in a dark vault would have little charm
for imagination. We none of us wish to be

[1] Marvin, *Last Words of Distinguished Men and Women*,
edition of 1902, p. 44.

buried sitting in a rocking-chair or reclining in
a bed. All these and many other capricious
and whimsical fancies are not only not attractive but positively repellant to most men.
And yet we are, no doubt, already making
elaborate preparation for entombment. We
desire a marble sarcophagus or a granite shaft.
We are putting aside money for the care of the
lot in the cemetery. We would like to have a
rose-bush planted by the headstone. If we
prefer cremation, we are anxious with regard
to the urn. We want our ashes mingled with
the ashes of some dear friend. Dr. Samuel
Parr, the great English scholar and critic, left
a paper labelled, "Directions for my Funeral."
He described the kind of burial he wanted,
the order and character of the procession, the
nature of the service, and the names of the
clergymen who were to be invited. He selected
the persons who were to act as bearers. He
even went so far as to name the maker of his
coffin. He wrote:

"I lay particular stress upon the following re-
quests: My hands must be bound by the crape
hat-band which I wore at the burial of my daughter
Catherine: upon my breast must be placed a piece
of flannel which Catherine wore at her dying moments at Teignmouth. There must be a lock of
Madelina's hair enclosed in silk, and wrapped in

14

paper, bearing her name: there must be a lock of Catherine's hair in silk and paper with her name: there must be a lock of my late wife's hair, preserved in the same way: there must be a lock of Sarah Wynne's hair, preserved in the same way. All these locks of hair must be laid on my bosom, as carefully as possible, covered and fastened with a piece of black silk to keep them together."

Jeremy Bentham wished to have his skeleton preserved, and he directed Dr. Smith to cause the bones to be articulated, clothed in a black suit, and seated in a chair. He wanted the bony hand to grasp a gold-headed cane. The philosopher desired to break down a strong prejudice then existing against the dissection of human bodies; and so, in the disposal of his own body, he planned a *post mortem* campaign against what he regarded as a gross and injurious superstition. John Ziska gave orders that a drum should be made out of his skin. Shouting hosts followed Ziska's resounding integument, and wherever the drum went victory followed. Voltaire addressed some interesting lines on the subject of the Ziska drum to Frederick II. of Prussia:

" And is it true?   Did you indeed
From Austrian or Bohemian win
The drum which dying Ziska bade
Them manufacture from his skin?

" A dead man's hide is little worth,
      Though, when alive, a hero he:
   Your heroes do not oft escape
      The worm's unmanner'd gluttony.

" To hide of Ziska Fate decreed
      Nor worm nor reptile should lay claim;
   But should through ages be preserv'd
      In drum immortal as his name.

" 'T was odd enough!   But pray be pleas'd,
      O mighty king! to understand—
   Your hero, who would save his hide,
      Must condescend to have it tann'd.

" Sire, keep your own; for God Himself,
      Who drew it on thus well to fit,
   Could scarcely, should He try once more,
      A new one fill so full of wit! "
            Translated by THOMAS HOLCROFT.

Robert, King of Scotland, vowed that in the
event of his succeeding in his military opera-
tions he would go to the East and fight against
"the adversaries of the Christian faith."   He
was distressed in mind during his last sickness
because he had not accomplished his heart's
desire.   He was about to die, and could not
take up arms against the enemies of his Lord
and Saviour.   In his extremity he requested
the brave Douglas to remove his heart from

his body so soon as life was extinct, and to deposit it in the Holy Sepulchre. Douglas endeavored to discharge the commission, and every one knows with what result.

The self-absorption of Marie Bashkirtseff centred in a desire to be thought of and talked about after her death. She lived with the to-morrow of death always before her. She vowed that if God would satisfy her ambition, which was certainly neither altruistic nor noble, she would go upon a pilgrimage. The vow was made when she was fifteen years old. At nineteen she decided that she would no longer ask the help of God. Still later she reflected that "prayer is better than anything else for stirring the emotions," and so she returned to a somewhat religious life. She prepared her *Journal of a Young Artist* with the one purpose of creating for herself an enduring monument. Madame Bashkirtseff certainly understood her daughter's spirit and ambition when she constructed close to the entrance of the rural cemetery of Passy the monument of white stone so massive and decorative in effect. The monument is divided into two parts— vault and chapel. The latter is fitted up like a studio that has just been quitted by the artist. It contains Marie's rocking-chair, table, favorite books. On the walls are inscribed in

letters of gold the names of her paintings, and
lines by Coppée and other poets who knew
and admired the young Russian girl.   In the
vault stands the sarcophagus covered with
flowers, and on the wall is a life-size portrait
of Marie.

Men are unwilling to relax their hold upon
the activities of this world even in the grave.
If they cannot live themselves, they insist that
their names and influence shall continue.
They name cities and streets after themselves.
They write books and paint pictures for posterity.   Thousands of men subsist upon the *post
mortem* ambitions and desires of their fellow-
men.   Colleges are endowed and professorships
are named by men who cling to the hope of immortality.   Take from the human mind dread
of oblivion, and there would be comparatively
few cadets at West Point.   Whoever shall in
the years to come succeed in rendering the
world indifferent to the future, will have it in
his power to pauperize Oxford, Cambridge,
Harvard, Yale, and Columbia Universities.
Centuries ago Horace boasted that he had
builded in his deathless poems "a monument
more enduring than brass;" and to-day thousands of scribblers for magazines and papers
cherish the same ambition and indulge the
same dream.

Is the hope of immortality in the race an unworthy and trivial thing? Would men be better in heart and life were they reconciled to the thought of annihilation? Even Auguste Comte knew better. Read his touching farewell to Clotilde de Vaux:

"Thy celestial inspiration will dominate the remainder of my life, public as well as private, and preside over my progress toward perfection, purifying my sentiments, ennobling my thoughts, and elevating my conduct. Perhaps, as the principal reward of the grand tasks yet left me to contemplate and complete under thy powerful invocation, I shall inseparably unite thy name with my own in the latest remembrances of a grateful humanity."

The distinguished Frenchman did not believe in the immortality of the human soul, and yet he hoped to be loved and remembered by posterity; and he wished to have his name and that of the beautiful and gifted Clotilde de Vaux inscribed together in the imperishable regard of mankind. I spent a never-to-beforgotten afternoon with Walt Whitman not many years before he died, and the one impression made by that interview upon my mind was that of Whitman's constant thought of the future. He was as avaricious of enduring fame as was Comte.

Goethe was for a moment staggered by the thought of the afterwards of death. "To me," said he, "the thought of a life without end, even though it were a happy one, appears more dreadful than the most acute physical anguish." The great poet forgot the capacity of the human mind for infinite development, and that not even eternity can exhaust its power. A noted mathematician has calculated that in solving the possible problems of plain circles alone, one could spend seven hundred million years. Is it, then, difficult to understand how an eternity might be employed in the acquisition of knowledge? When Socrates said to the weeping friends who gathered around him after he had received the fatal cup, "You may bury me if you can catch me," he anticipated for his immortal part another life worthy of his philosophical attainments. It was his comfort in the hour of death to know that he should spend eternity in the society of great and gifted men like Hesiod and Homer. Such society seemed to him well calculated to make immortality a priceless boon.

AN UNAMBITIOUS GENIUS

MY thoughts revert this evening to a dear friend of many years ago. The battle of life was too hard for his delicate and nervous temperament, and he died in the early morning of youth. Men called him romantic and impracticable, sensitive and quite too high-strung for his humble place and still more humble prospects. But I, who knew him well, can bear testimony to the generous and noble qualities of his heart, and to the superiority of his mind, which, even at so early a period in life, was enriched with a most unusual store of learning. He never matriculated in any college, and yet could read Latin and Greek classics in the original, and could read them well. My library, which was not large at that time, was the only one to which he had access, and yet he was thoroughly acquainted with the best work of English, American, German, and French writers. How he came by his knowledge of many rare books, especially in foreign languages, I could never discover. He gave promise of developing into a poet and philosopher of no mean order, and yet to-day not a person beyond the border of his native town knows that he ever lived; and so utterly perished is his memory from the face of the earth that, when, not long ago, I visited his grave, I found the headstone fallen upon the sod with the inscription under, so that name and date of death could be no longer read.

All this is certainly very sad to think of, and yet I am sure it would not have troubled my friend could he have looked far enough into the future to have seen his grave thus miserably neglected. It never disturbed him that his genius was unrecognized, nor did he care that all his learning was wasted upon an unappreciative circle of rustic boors. He was absolutely without ambition, and was satisfied with the present enjoyment of what he knew and could do. He read, studied, and composed verses and essays, simply for the pleasure which he found in literary work, and without any thought of winning thereby a name among men. Nor did he care to turn his genius and scholarship to financial ends. I secured him an engagement with a city journal, but the editor, applying to him for "copy," received nothing in return but an indignant expostulation. His absorbing delight was in literary

work, and yet he never exaggerated the value
of such work, nor did he think himself one
whit better than the most ill-informed of his
neighbors. Indeed, he once broke into the
most rapturous praise of an old shoemaker who
had provided him with a pair of perfect-fitting
leather slippers, and I remember that he aston-
ished the cobbler by likening him to one of
Homer's heroes. He was upon the best of
terms with a blacksmith whose skill he envied,
and once he said: "It is true I can read Latin
and Greek and make verses in three languages,
but all that and much more is as nothing when
compared with the skill of Jack Dolan. When
he stirs the fire and swings the sledge-hammer,
I see old Vulcan on earth again. I believe
there is no greater man in all the world than a
good blacksmith." The village pastor asked
him to teach in the Sunday-school, and two
weeks later discovered that he had consumed
all the time that should have been given to religious instruction in acquainting youngsters
with the arts of hunting and trapping.

When the good man remonstrated with my
friend, and spoke to him of the superior importance of spiritual things, concluding the
admonition with the statement that, however
valuable a knowledge of the natural and visible
world might be, the man himself was of vastly

more consequence, the young poet composed
and forwarded to the manse the following
lines:

" Man, beast, and every leafy tree,
　·And all the world beside,
　From thine own brooding thought have sprung,
　And in thy dream abide.

" Should'st thou awake and view thyself
　No longer one with these,
　As summer clouds they must depart,
　And as the evening breeze.

" Passion, and pride, and shame, and grief,
　And wisdom vast and grand,
　Obedient rise with thy desire,—
　Dissolve at thy command.

" Why should'st thou fret, and pine, and grieve,
　By thine own soul deceived,
　Since life, and death, and thine own self,
　Thou hast thyself conceived?

" Let gladness wing the passing hour;
　Ye anxious cares, subside!
　Be decked with flowers, ye isles of green,
　'Mid life's encircling tide!

" And when at last the shadows fall,
　And darkness veils the day,
　Dreamer and dream alike shall cease,
　And time shall pass away."

The pastor was grieved, and wrote the young man a letter as sad as it was kind, and full of the deepest solicitude for the spiritual welfare of a gifted but erring soul. This touched the conscience in a tender place, and drew forth another poem in atonement for the heretical lines that had so wounded the heart of a truly good and pious man. And now, after thirty-five years, I unfold the creased and time-stained manuscript, and read again these verses:

" This world may be ' a fleeting show,
    For man's illusion given,'
  As sang the bard of long ago—
    And be his song forgiven.

" And man himself, a cloud-wreath blown
    Athwart the summer sky,
  May have nor grace nor strength to live
    Before 't is time to die.

" Yet holy men have bravely poured
    Their blood like purple wine,
  The circling years to glorify
    With radiancy divine.

" They braced them for the shock of war,
    Where right and wrong contend;
  And God Himself was on the field,
    To strengthen and defend.

" Yes, saint and sage, with loving heart,
    Have fought for you and me,—
To make the great world glad and good,
    As God would have it be."

I candidly confess that my friend was not to
all men at all times an agreeable companion.
He had the uncomfortable habit of speaking
the truth, or what he thought the truth, in
a most unconventional way. For whatever of
sentiment and feeling, both in the works
of great authors and in the common lives of
ordinary men, was artificial or unreal, he had
the most unqualified hatred. I once heard
him say that an honest and healthy mind could
as easily extract pleasure from the miserable
side of life as could bees draw honey from
deadly poisons. Certainly, much of the en-
vironment of his earthly existence was anything but attractive, from my point of view;
and yet in it all he rejoiced, pouring the wealth
of a peculiarly gifted mind and womanly sensitiveness of heart into all that was most dull,
prosaic, and monotonous. No one who had
only a superficial acquaintance with him could
have suspected how delicately constructed was
his nervous system. He himself did not know
how interwoven in his own nature were the
elements of strength and weakness. Life was

to him a perpetual delight, and yet, when the death hour came, he passed on in quietness of soul to what he described as "the heavenly surprise."

I treasure among my most precious books my young friend's copy of Horace, upon a fly-leaf of which are these lines in his delicate chirography, and which are, to my mind, highly characteristic:

> " Thanks be to God who made us all,
> That we shall neither stand nor fall
> By man's opinion."

SUCCESS

SIR FRANCIS HASTINGS DOYLE (1813–1885) has given the world an unusually attractive book in his *Reminiscences and Opinions*. During a long life he enjoyed intimate acquaintance with many of the most eminent Englishmen. He was a friend and schoolmate, at Eton, of Gladstone and Arthur Hallam, and records many recollections of their debates together. He was also with them at Oxford, where he was afterward a fellow. Later he became a barrister, but was forced by poverty, soon after his marriage, to enter the civil service, and was thus excluded from active Parliamentary life. In 1867 he was elected Professor of Poetry at Oxford, and some of his lectures there have been published. At the close of a life covering more than seventy years, he confesses with wonderful frankness that he has lacked that definite aim and steadfast purpose which, with his natural abilities and education, might have secured him a high place in literature or politics. A sad confession,

and one not wholly justified by the results
of his life. His friendships, companionships,
attainments, and position at Oxford, all placed
before us in his own most attractive English,
are a sufficient answer to the severe charge
which he brings against himself. What is success? Doubtless a hundred men would answer
the question in as many different ways. One
man's success is another's failure. He who
acquires ten thousand dollars may be far
wealthier than the envied possessor of millions. He who holds the realization of his
highest ideal essential to success must be content either to cherish a poor ideal or to inscribe
"failure" over his best endeavors. We all
come short of our possibilities and dreams, but
it by no means follows that life is a failure.
Success must be measured by the grand result
rather than by the far-away ideal.

There is no royal road to success. "Short
cuts" end in failure. They who enter not by
the door, but climb up some other way, are, to
say the least, questionable adventurers. Attention to details is the doorway through
which genius enters the enchanted land of
beauty. Said Michael Angelo, "Little things
make perfection, but perfection is not a little
thing." Meissonier's thoroughness is sometimes marvellous, and becomes painful to

behold. It is said that he will never allow a
picture to leave his studio unless he is satisfied
that it represents the best work possible to
him at the time. A crowd of amateurs and
dealers may be found in his studio bidding
almost like men in an auction-room for the
work as it stands unfinished on the easel.
"You will let me have that." "No; you
promised it to me." Meissonier lets them
talk on; and presently he takes up a palette-
knife and effaces, with one scrape, the principal
figure. There is a cry of horror, and the artist
is left alone to recommence the struggle for
perfection. It is not often that he is satisfied
with the first execution of a picture, and some
of his canvases have remained for years on their
easels, awaiting the final touch of his brush.
When building his house he had it torn partly
down eight times, because some insignificant
detail displeased him. I knew of a clergyman
who would never permit a blot, an erasure, or
an altered line to disfigure the perfect pages of
his often faultless sermons. He would rewrite
a sermon ten or twelve times. Joubert was
constantly haunted by the desire to condense
all he had written into a single line. He said:
"If there be a man plagued with the accursed
ambition of putting a whole volume into a
page, a whole page into a sentence, and that

15

sentence into a word, it is I." He believed
that whatever was worth doing was worth
doing well. Of Edgar Allan Poe a biographer
writes:

" He was painfully alive to all imperfections of
art; and a false rhyme, an ambiguous sentence, or
even a typographical error, threw him into an
ecstacy of passion. It was this sensitiveness to all
artistic imperfections, rather than any malignity of
feeling, which made his criticism so severe, and
procured him a host of enemies among persons
toward whom he never entertained any personal ill-
will. He criticised his own productions with the
same severity that he exercised toward the writings
of others."

Little things make perfection not in art and
literature only, but in all departments of life.
The artist who misplaced a single tile spoiled
the mosaic. A unit more or less will change
the entire result.

Authors are not infrequently discouraged
because they fail of immediate success. They
cannot wait. The popular novel may outsell
a book of real worth, but the latter will outlive
the former. When the author of the ephemeral
story has been long forgotten, the writer of
the more substantial volume will continue to
live, and the labor of his mind will " bear fruit

in old age." Let no one be discouraged by
the indifference of either publishers or the
reading world. Let each man give the age
the best there is in him. Let the noblest word
be spoken, even though it die in immediate
silence with no suggestion of an echo. There
was sold at auction in London a letter from
Browning to a young poet who wrote asking
Browning's advice about publishing a volume
of poems. The reply, in part, is as follows:
"It sounds strange and almost sad to me that
I should be imagined of authority in this kind,
I who for years could not get a line printed
except at my own expense, and I began half a
century ago or more." So also was it with
Thoreau who in 1847 wrote thus to Emerson,
who was at the time in England:

"I suppose you will like to hear of my book,
though I have nothing worth writing about it. Indeed, for the last month or two I have forgotten it,
but shall certainly remember it again. Wiley and
Putnam, Munroe, the Harpers, and Crosby and
Nichols have all declined printing it with the least
risk to themselves ; but Wiley and Putnam will
print it in their series, and any of them, anywhere,
at *my* risk."

Ruskin had his experience. Emerson's essay
on *Nature* was at first a failure from the pub-

lisher's point of view.   Its sale during the first
twelve years of its printed existence averaged
but one copy for every ten days.   Whitman's
Leaves of Grass fought for every breath it was
permitted to draw for many a year.   Neglect
should not greatly disturb the sincere mind.
The public may crave carob-pods, and publishers may be greedy for the shekels derived from
the sale of such provender, but in the end the
true and the beautiful must survive.   The
great future must be trusted for vindication
and reward.

WILLIAM PARKER SNOW

I HAVE often thought I should like to say a word or two about a friend of my boyhood days whose daring adventures were known to the last generation, and whose books were read a half-century ago. One of the most interesting men I ever knew was William Parker Snow, an English sea-captain and Arctic discoverer, who was for a time in charge of the mission yacht *Allen Gardiner*. In him were strangely mingled the spirit of wild adventure and the enthusiastic love of all that is beautiful in art and letters.

I came to know him when I was a child. He lived for about a year in a hut on the edge of a dense forest, far up on the hill upon the slope of which is builded the village of Nyack. My father was at the time pastor of the Reformed Church in that village, and I was a schoolboy living in my father's home, and preparing myself for college. Why Captain Snow remained so long at Nyack, and why his dwelling was so primitive, I never

229

knew; but his presence in the village for one whole year led to a close acquaintance and friendship that had marked influence upon my mental development.

It was during that year—I think it was 1867 —he wrote his book, *Lee and His Generals*, not one of his best books, but still a work of no little merit. The Captain had seen the world. He had wintered amid the everlasting snows of the polar regions, and had penetrated into the dense jungles of tropical lands; he had lived with savages, and had fought with cannibals hand to hand for his life; and he had been shipwrecked upon unknown and inhospitable shores. His life was everything that appealed to the imagination of a youth naturally inclined to the romantic side of human experience and fond of books, with a great longing in his heart for travel and the world. And the Captain, pleased, I suppose, with the worship of a young man, and delighted with the opportunity of helpfully directing in some measure the effort and enthusiasm of an eager and inquiring mind, gave himself apparently without reserve to the gracious work of enlarging that youth's mental horizon, and stimulating within him a love for noble things. As I look back and remember the conceit and waywardness of my early days I am sure my good friend must have been a man of unusual patience and kindness of heart.

There came a time when the Captain's literary work in the little hut at Nyack was finished. Then he went his way. The youth grew to man's estate and became a minister of the Gospel in the Congregational Church, but never was there effaced from his mind the impression received from that one marvellous year of revelation.

Twenty years later, after a few months of rest and travel upon the Continent, I found myself in London. Passing Exeter Hall one morning, I stopped to read the bulletin board. There was the name of my old friend of whom I had heard nothing, save through notices of his books, for so long a time: "The Bishop of London will address this afternoon the Annual Meeting of the South American Missionary Society. Capt. W. Parker Snow will give an account of his life among savage peoples." It is needless to say that no time was lost in renewing the old acquaintance. I heard the Captain's address. It was the speech of a bluff, genuine English sailor, but it had in it the same reverence for both moral and artistic beauty. The voice was somewhat broken, but it had all the old enthusiasm and tenderness. Age had whitened his hair and wrinkled his

brow, but had not in the least abated his courage. Yet time had brought to him a touch of
sadness, for he missed the active and public
life to which he had been so long accustomed;
and he could not understand why the English
Government was unwilling to trust him with
a new command upon the sea. He was old,
but he did not know it. The last time I saw
my friend it was at his home on Victoria Road,
Bexley Heath, in Kent. All the afternoon we
sat together in his library and talked of the
early days and of the beautiful shores of the
Hudson. He loved America and longed to
return and visit it once more. When there
was a pause in the conversation he took from
a shelf the books he had written, and told me
why and how he had written them. I remember that he patted the covers of his *Voyage of
the 'Prince Albert' in Search of Sir John Franklin ;* it was a narrative of life in the Arctic seas,
and its pages made him young again, as in the
days when he endured the silence and solitude
of the long winter night in the frozen world
of the far North. He handled with almost
equal affection his *Two Years' Cruise off Terra
del Fuego, the Falkland Islands, and the Sea-
board of Patagonia.* He was not mistaken in
thinking the book had some enduring qualities,
for I have since seen a review of it in the *Lon-*

don Athenæum that gave it no small measure of praise.

His *Catalogue of the Arctic Collection in the British Museum*, which made its appearance in 1858, did not seem to interest him; and I do not remember that he commented at all upon his *British Columbia Emigration*, and his *Lee and His Generals*, a copy of which lies before me, with a number of letters written by him to me after my return to the United States folded between the leaves. It was a delightful afternoon and the situation of his house was most attractive. From the library window we could look far over the fields to the distant hills. But I do not think he cared much for the landscape—his thoughts were with the sea.

A jug of ale and a loaf of dark bread, which he cut with a case-knife, served for repast—it was better suited to his life and to our brief hour of fellowship than the most elaborate entertainment could have been. I knew we should never meet upon this earth again, but the thought, while it added tenderness to our interview, did not sadden me. My friend's work was done, and the evening twilight was falling. The Captain had no pipe, and there were no "wreaths of fragrant smoke," but somehow whenever I recall that afternoon with my friend in his English home, Edward

FitzGerald's lines run softly through my mind
like a remembered tune:

" Then go we to smoking,
    Silent and snug:
Naught passes between us,
    Save a brown jug—
            Sometimes!

" And sometimes a tear
    Will rise in each eye,
Seeing the two old friends
    So merrily—
            So merrily! "

I first learned of the Captain's death from
a bookseller's catalogue in which collectors of
rare and curious works were offered, "The
Author's Own Copy of *Voyage of the 'Prince
Albert' in Search of Sir John Franklin*, with
four colored plates, a few extra plates and
maps, and in addition the autograph correspondence with him (thirty-two letters) of
Arctic explorers and seamen." The dealer
had also for sale " Notes and a Copious MS.
Index by the Author, and two pamphlets by
him on the *Prince Albert's* track through the
ice of Baffin's Bay; with letters written to him
at various times by Lady Franklin, John Bar-
row, Lord Northbrook, Adml. Sir Francis

Beaufort, Lord Macaulay and others, with a few Arctic Relics."

When I saw the bookseller's cold-blooded announcement I softly closed the mercenary pages and whispered to myself:

" Yet with the falling leaves,
    Sweet friendship cannot die."

THE RELIGIOUS SIGNIFICANCE OF
PRECIOUS STONES

PRECIOUS stones have a psychological or
moral interest growing out of early association with mental and spiritual qualities and
concerns. Thus we find the New Jerusalem
(Revelation xxi., 18–21) resplendent with
jewels, each stone being emblematic:

" The building of the wall thereof was jasper;
and the city was pure gold, like unto pure glass.
The foundations of the wall of the city were
adorned with all manner of precious stones. The
first foundation was jasper; the second, sapphire
(lapis lazuli); the third, chalcedony; the fourth,
emerald; the fifth, sardonyx; the sixth, sardius;
the seventh, chrysolite; the eighth, beryl; the
ninth, topaz; the tenth, chrysoprase; the eleventh,
jacinth (or sapphire); the twelfth, amethyst.
And the twelve gates were twelve pearls; each one
of the several gates was of one pearl; and the
street of the city was pure gold, as it were transparent glass (or transparent as glass)."

Jeremy Taylor turns the apocalyptic vision into verse:

" What ravished heart, seraphic tongue, or eyes
    Clear as the morning rise,
    Can speak, or think, or see
    That bright eternity,
Where the great king's transparent throne
Is of an entire jasper stone?
    There the eye
    O' the chrysolite,
    And a sky
Of diamonds, rubies, chrysoprase—
And, above all, Thy holy face—

    " Makes an eternal charity.
When Thou Thy jewels up dost bind, that day
Remember us, we pray—
    That where the beryl lies,
    And the crystal 'bove the skies,
There Thou mayest appoint us place
Within the brightness of Thy face—
    And our soul
    In the scroll
    Of life and blissfulness enroll,
That we may praise Thee to eternity.   Alleluia! "

The thoughtful reader will call to mind Byron's lines beginning with, "I saw the city of the skies," and also the description of Ecbatana found in Herodotus.   The New Jerusalem

is symbolical. A walled city gives us ideas of
security and society. The walls are seven, and
may signify the seven virtues: faith, hope,
charity (the first three are called "holy
virtues")—the "charity" is now translated
"love" (1 Cor. xiii., 13),—prudence, justice,
fortitude, and temperance. The number seven
symbolizes the gifts of the Spirit (Rev. i., 12)
and has a religious purport throughout both
Testaments. We have "Seven Mortal Sins,"
"Seven Sorrows of Mary," "Seven Utterances
of Christ on the Cross," and the "Seven-Hilled
City." The jasper of Revelation is thought to
be diamond, the moral of which is innocence,
durability, and value. Sapphire means repentance, and is used to signify the heavenly faith
of St. Andrew. Chalcedony is emblematic of
purity and is St. James's stone. Emerald is
emblematic of youth and gentleness, and is St.
John's stone. The sardonyx is friendship, and
when placed beside onyx gives us conjugal
felicity. Chrysolite is pure as sunshine. Beryl
is doubting faith and stands for Thomas.
Topaz is delicacy. Chrysoprase means serenity and trustfulness. Jacinth is constancy,
fidelity, and a sweet temper. An old myth
tells us how, when Adam fell, a jacinth of
extreme whiteness dropped from heaven and
lodged upon the earth. Its brightness dazzled

the eyes at a distance of even four days' journey. Amethyst stands for sobriety. Condor, describing the heavenly city in his *Harmony of History and Prophecy*, says: "The precious stones of which the walls of the holy city appeared to consist, whatever mystical or symbolical significance may attach to them, are obviously intended to describe the color of each resplendent elevation; and, although the colors do not occur in the precise prismatic order, the combination would have the general effect of a double rainbow." Thus beautifully Wordsworth describes the glory of the city of jewelled walls and golden streets:

> " The appearance, instantaneously disclosed,
> Was of a mighty city—boldly say
> A wilderness of building, sinking far,
> And self-withdrawn into a wondrous depth,
> Far sinking into splendor without end!
> Fabric it seemed of diamond and of gold,
> With alabaster domes and silver spires,
> And blazing terrace upon terrace, high
> Uplifted: here, serene pavilions bright
> In avenues disposed: there towers begirt
> With battlements, that on their restless fronts
> Bore stars—illumination of all gems."

Quarles tells us:

> " Her streets with burnish'd gold are pavèd round;
> Stars lie like pebbles scattered on the ground;

Pearl mixt with onyx, and the jasper stone,
Made gravell'd causeways to be trampled on."

In the same spirit sings the good Bernard of
Cluny:

" With jasper glow thy bulwarks,
    Thy streets with emerald blaze;
The sardius and the topaz
    Unite in thee their rays;
Thine ageless walls are bonded
    With amethyst unpriced;
The saints build up its fabric,
    The corner-stone is Christ."

The hymnology treating of the New Jerusalem will repay the most careful study, and the
student may find valuable help in a little book
entitled *O Mother Dear, Jerusalem*, by William C. Prime (A. D. F. Randolph, New York,
1865), in which is given the entire poem so
named, with its history and several of its ver-
sions. The original of the poem, which is to
be found in the British Museum, dates from
the time of Queen Elizabeth. Three stanzas
set forth the jewelry of heaven:

" Thy walls are made of precious stones,
    Thy bulwarks diamonds square,
Thy gates are of right orient pearl,
    Exceeding rich and rare.

" Thy turrets and thy pinnacles,
    With carbuncles do shine,
Thy very streets are paved with gold,
    Surpassing clear and fine.

" Thy houses are of ivory,
    Thy windows crystal clear,
Thy tiles are made of beaten gold,
    O God, that I were there! "

The sapphire, which varies from a dark, rich blue to a pale and almost colorless tinge of the same hue, holds the next place in hardness to the diamond.   It is found in comparatively large masses in Ava and Ceylon.   The earliest mention of it is in Exodus xxiv., 10: "They saw the God of Israel, and there was under his feet as it were a paved work of sapphire-stone, and as it were the body of heaven in his clearness." It was the second stone in the second row of the high priest's breast-plate.   The lustre of the stone is not overestimated, allowing for poetical license, in the celebrated lines of Gray:

" The living throne, the sapphire blaze,
    Where angels tremble while they gaze,
    He saw; but, blasted with excess of light,
Closed his eyes in endless night.
                    Progress of Poesy.

The twelve apostles, who were poor enough
16

when they were in the flesh, are now each provided with a gem, and thus tricked out in ecclesiastical jewelry:

"Andrew — the bright blue *sapphire*, emblematic of his heavenly faith.

"Bartholomew—the red *cornelian*, emblematic of his martyrdom.

"James—the white *chalcedony*, emblematic of his purity.

"James the Less—the *topaz*, emblematic of delicacy.

"John—the *emerald*, emblematic of his youth and gentleness.

"Matthew—the *amethyst*, emblematic of sobriety. Matthew was a reformed 'publican,' and the amethyst dispels drunkenness.

"Matthias—the *chrysolite*, pure as sunshine.

"Peter—the *jasper*, hard and solid as the rock of the church.

"Philip—the friendly *sardonyx*.

"Simeon of Cana—the pink *hyacinth*, emblematic of sweet temper.

"Thaddeus — the *chrysoprase*, emblematic of serenity and trustfulness.

"Thomas—the *beryl*, indefinite in lustre, emblematic of his doubting faith."

Excerpted from *The Reader's Handbook*.

Apostle-rings and charms contain the twelve gems dedicated to the members of the Sacred

College.   These are sometimes set in a cross of
gold or silver.   The emerald, representing the
youth and gentleness of the beloved disciple,
is placed at the point where the beams cover
each other, and is often made more prominent
than the other stones in the crucifix.   The
emerald is a very fortunate gem, cementing
friendship and insuring constancy.   The topaz,
given to St. James the Less, is supposed to
check hemorrhages and promote digestion.
The amethyst, St. Matthew's stone, is called
the "prelate's gem," or "*pierre d'évêque,*" because set in the pastoral ring given to the
bishop in the Roman Catholic Church.

Queen Victoria's crown contained upward of
three thousand precious stones, mostly diamonds taken from old crowns.   These were
reset and arranged by Rundell and Bridges in
1838.   The principal diamonds may be tabu-
lated thus:

20 Diamonds round the circle, worth	£30,000
2 Large centre diamonds	4,000
54 Smaller diamonds at the angle	100
4 Large diamonds on the top of the crosses	40,000
25 Diamonds composing four crosses	12,000
12 Diamonds contained in fleur-de-lis	10,000
18 Smaller diamonds in the same	2,000
Pearls and smaller diamonds on arches and crosses	10,000
141 Small diamonds	500
26 Diamonds in the upper cross	3,000
2 Circles of pearls about the rim	300

In addition to the above the crown contains 1 large ruby of rare dimension, 16 sapphires, 4 small rubies, 1 large sapphire, 11 emeralds, 1363 brilliants, 273 pearls, 147 table diamonds, 4 drop-shaped pearls. The imperial state crown of England is one of the most beautiful and costly of all the European diadems.

Pearls, though not to be catalogued among precious stones, are highly valued for their beauty and are extensively used in all kinds of jewelry. They are the secretion of certain marine and fresh-water molluscs. The semi-transparent films, called *nacre* or mother-of-pearl, lining the shells, are cut and carved into various ornaments. The pearls, so-called, are the results of accident, and are grains of sand or spicules of shell heavily covered with the secretion. The Chinese introduce shot between the shell and the mantle of the fresh-water mussel, *Unis hyria*, and so obtain a large number of pearls without the danger of diving. They also insert little metallic images of the Buddha which are soon coated with pearl secretion and united with the shell. Linnæus obtained pearls by boring holes in the shell of a river mussel, and dropping in grains of sand. The ancients thought that pearls were drops of dew which, having fallen into the open shell, were changed by the mussel into the beautiful

gem they so greatly prized. Moore alludes to
the belief:

"And precious the tear as that rain from the sky
Which turns into pearls as it falls in the sea."

The most famous fishery is a bank thirty
miles long and from fifteen to twenty miles off
the shore of Ceylon. The season lasts three
months, commencing with February. The
divers remain under water from forty to
seventy seconds. The shore is covered with
shells for many miles, the result of more than
two thousand years of pearl-fishing. The
"which is frozen of" Job xxviii., 18, is translated in the authorized version, "pearls," but
may mean crystals. Pliny describes a pearl
which would be worth £80,000. The pearl Cleopatra swallowed, dissolved in wine, at the banquet given in honor of Antony, was valued at
£80,729. Æsopus, son of Claudius Æsopus,
the actor, swallowed a pearl said to have been
priceless. Sir Thomas Gresham was not to be
outdone by either of the classic celebrities; he
powdered a pearl valued at £15,000 and drank
it in a glass of wine as a health to Queen Elizabeth, and to win a wager with the ambassador
from Spain that he would give a more costly
banquet than was ever given by a Spaniard.

" Here fifteen thousand pounds at one clap goes
Instead of sugar; Gresham drinks the pearl
Unto his queen and mistress."
THOMAS HEYWOOD.

An old Roman author mentions a string of
pearls worth one million sesterces, or £8000
sterling. The pearl in the possession of the
Emperor of Persia was purchased in 1633, and
is believed to be worth £110,400. Philip II.
had a pearl the size of a pigeon's egg, and
costing fourteen thousand four hundred ducats.
The "Incomparable" is said to be as large as a
muscadine pear, and is described by De Boote
as weighing thirty carats. An Oriental poet,
impressed, no doubt, with the exceeding great
value of some pearl like the "Incomparable,"
or like the marvellous possession of the Emperor of Persia, sums the matter up, so far as
he is concerned, in a couplet addressed to his
lady :

"A giant mussel is this world, I said,
And thou a single pearl within it laid."

ETERNITY IN AN HOUR

NOW that every house has its clock and every man his watch, are not our days "cut and hacked wretchedly into small portions?" Are not our lives in danger of becoming entirely mechanical under the constant swinging of pendulums and uncoiling of mainsprings? It is the time-element that impoverishes work; and he who obsequiously complies with the humors of men, fulfilling the letter rather than the spirit, is correctly called a time-server. The best things cannot be finished to order in a given period of time. Michael Angelo must work when the spirit is upon him. Great frescos and cathedrals grow out of minds that conceive and execute them, as trees rise from the earth. He who would perform his task well must make of it no task at all. Count time as you please—by lunar, solar, sidereal, or tropical years—and it is the same; one year is as good as another. Any one of them might as well end in June as in December. The boundary lines are imaginary, and every mo-

ment marks the expiration of twelve months
"No rising sun but lights a new year." December comes to an end, and, at midnight, the
sun completes its revolution through the eclip-
tic, and the earth its circuit round the sun;
but faith hears no song in the heavens, and
science discovers no clicking of celestial machinery and no rush of aërial currents. As
ships cross lines of latitude and longitude without experiencing any change in temperature,
so the ship of human life sails over the years
and marks not the passage. And how variable
and unreliable is human perception in this
matter. Have as many clocks and watches as
you please, still "we live in feelings, not in
figures on a dial, and count time by heart-
throbs." We believe our own pulses against
all the chronometers in the world. We may
whisper to ourselves, "There are but sixty
minutes in the hour," nevertheless happy
hours fly and sad ones creep. The poet strives

" To see a world in a grain of sand,
   And a heaven in a wild flower:
   Hold infinity in the palm of his hand,
   And eternity in an hour."

Many a sorrowful heart has found eternity in
less than an hour. The criminal awaiting
execution may live through vast ages in a

single second. A sailor, escaped from the perils of shipwreck, described his twenty-four hours upon a floating spar as longer than all the years of his life. As the infant, opening its eyes in mingled wonder, fear, and delight to the changing scenes of this busy world, has no idea of either time or space, but reaches out its little hands to grasp the distant moon, and is impatient of every delay in the gratification of its fancies, so the dying, who measure the flying moments, not by "figures on a dial," but by heart-throbs and tear-drops, sometimes lose all sense of time just before they pass from it into eternity. Time is but another name for those little divisions we make in eternity, and eternity is the expanse of God's infinite existence. The hours, days, weeks, months, years, centuries, and millenniums are but faint shadows upon the glowing disc of His vast duration. Consider the magnitude of time. An hour is exhaustless. No one ever emptied a second. As animalculæ swim without sense of confinement in a drop of water, so our lives float in the present moment. We never live in more than one second at a time, and yet we experience no constraint and have all the space we require. We cry for more time, and cannot dispose of what we already have. We possess not too little, but too much;

we waste what we have.   We nibble at an hour,
and then leave it for another, as a mouse gnaws
at a cheese many times its size, and which it
cannot devour.   Men are praying for eternity
who wasted yesterday, and are utterly unable
to dispose of to-day.   Before the day arrives it
has no existence, and when it is over there
still remains to it no existence.   Thus are all
our marks upon the sand washed out by the
flowing tides of a sea no man may compass.
To one who has been dead a day it is practically the same to him, so far as this earth is
concerned, as if he had been in the grave a
hundred thousand centuries.   The shallowest
grave is bottomless; and yet into a grave so
deep the human soul looks with unshaken
confidence, and dares to exclaim, "This cor-
ruptible must put on incorruption, and this
mortal must put on immortality."

NEARING THE END OF THE JOURNEY

A S thoughtful men of pure life and sincere
purpose advance in years, they come to
see in the twilight of earthly existence many
things not visible at dawn nor in the blaze of
a meridian sun. When the shadows fall and
we near the end of the journey, we pitch our
tent and sit down in the opening to view the
landscape. Ambition no longer dazzles the
eye, and passion can no more excite the nerve.
Instead of enthusiasm we have experience.
God approaches the soul, and eternity appears
real. Thus it comes to pass that a man like
William Cullen Bryant, whose associations
were during most of his life with those who
deny the divine nature of our Saviour, viewing
spiritual things in the calm twilight, turns
away from other teachers to write thus lovingly
of the Lord:

" Take away the blessing of the advent of Christ's
life, and blessings purchased by His death, in what
an abyss of guilt would man have been left! It

would seem to be blotting the sun out of the heavens—to leave our system of worlds in chaos, frost, and darkness. In my view of the life, the teachings, the labors, and the sufferings of the blessed Jesus, there can be no admiration too profound, no love of which the human heart is capable too warm, no gratitude too earnest and deep of which He is justly the object. It is with sorrow that I confess my love for Him is so cold, and my gratitude so inadequate. It is with sorrow that I see any attempt to put aside His teachings as a delusion, to turn men's eyes from His example, to meet with doubt and denial the story of His life. For my part, if I thought that the religion of skepticism were to gather strength and prevail, and become the dominant view of mankind, I should despair of the fate of mankind in the years that are to come."

As George Ripley neared the boundary line that divides this world from that which lies before us, he too viewed spiritual things in a very different light from that in which they presented themselves to him earlier in life. Though a "radical" Unitarian and a leader among New England transcendentalists, he desired to spend the closing days of his remarkable life in the society of Evangelical Christian ministers. He turned away from Parker and Emerson to study the Word of

God, and in the simple hymns of Dr. Watts, inartistic most of them, and yet full of holy faith and love, he took great delight. We see things more nearly as they are when the heat and dust of life are over, but it is a sad reflection that then there remains little time for the correction of mistakes.

When one cuts himself loose from the truth of God in Christ, it is impossible to know through what thickets he will drag himself, or over what precipice he will at last leap into destruction. The lives of Harriet Martineau and "George Eliot" cannot be read without sadness. It is to be feared that the life of Frederic Harrison, the brilliant essayist of the *Fortnightly Review*, will furnish in time equally melancholy food for calm and dispassionate thought. No one need be surprised by this confession from Mr. Harrison:

" I passed through the ordinary stages of Broad Church, no Church, spirit of the Gospel, Natural Theology, Ontological haze, Philosophical Theism, the eternal-not-ourselves-that-make-for righteousness, the Unknowable, and most of the other substitutes for the Prayer Book and the Bible, seeking rest, and finding none; and a hollow, dismal, shifting country did I find it. All this time I had been reading Comte; and after some years of continual study, I slowly came to find solid ground in his conception of humanity as a practical Providence, and in the service of man as the practical sum of religion."

Hundreds and thousands of men have travelled over the same "hollow, dismal, shifting country," though not all have arrived at exactly the same terminus. Orestes A. Brownson passed through many forms of belief and disbelief to find himself at last the theologian of Roman Catholicism. Let a man doubt long enough and far enough and he shall either fall into the hopeless vortex of spiritual chaos, or be overtaken by the dense darkness of some colossal superstition. We know of nothing more shocking to an enlightened and sensitive conscience than to see an earnest soul, after a long and tempestuous voyage, drop anchor in the treacherous waters of some damnable lie.

OLD JEFF.

THIS morning (December 21, 1896) there died, in a queer little house on Church Street, in Great Barrington, a most quaint and picturesque colored man, whose chief delight was the distinction of being the oldest person in Berkshire County, and perhaps in all Massachusetts. No one can say with certainty what was his age, but it is known that he was born before 1789. It is the popular belief that he had seen a hundred and twelve summers; and surely, if his own computation, based upon certain dates in the family history of one of his old masters at the South, may be trusted, he was far beyond the century mark. His real name was Thomas Jefferson McKinley, but he was familiarly known to the inhabitants of Great Barrington as "Old Jeff." He was honest and kind; self-respecting, and respected by all who knew him. His blameless life of quiet rectitude was a rebuke to not a few well educated and prominent white men in his own village, whose crooked careers secured for them

neither public confidence or private regard.　In
addition to all this, he was by no means bad
company, when once his peculiar disposition
and mental characteristics were understood.
He was seldom dull or stupid to one who knew
how to engage his attention and draw upon his
exhaustless fund of homely information.　He
was, in a rude way, something of a philosopher,
and worked out to his own satisfaction many
knotty and vexatious problems, as he went
from house to house with his basket of small
fruits and fresh vegetables, all of which had
been raised in his own garden, and for which
he asked and received good prices.　Though
he had no education, in the common accepta-
tion of that word, still his intellectual vision
was remarkably clear, and his reasoning usually
brought him to correct results.　I once heard
him reprove a very intelligent white man for
wishing the old times back again.　He said:
"I was once a miserable slave in New Orleans,
and almost as ignorant as a dumb beast.　It
was only when I fell in with a South Berkshire
company of the Forty-ninth Massachusetts
Infantry, at Port Hudson, that I found out I
was a man.　Do you think I could wish those
long, degrading years of slavery back?　No,
freedom is much better than bondage, and,
therefore, the present is better than the past.

And you, also, my white friend, were once a slave, for you were subject, as I have heard, to some very false impressions, from which college and church have in a measure emancipated you. You are what you are because you no longer live in the past. When you wish for the past you are like the Israelites in the wilderness, crying out for the shame and slavery of Egypt. The best thing about the past is that it is gone forever; the best thing about the present is that it is going as rapidly as possible; and the best thing about the future is that it is always just a little ahead of us, so that we have to exert ourselves to reach after it.''

"Old Jeff" was only a "darky," and his external life was bare of all adornment, yet I believe he was wiser and more of a gentleman than are many well-dressed sons of luxury to whom, because they have a little social and political power, men bow down. He once expressed after the following fashion his idea of what it is to be a gentleman: "From the way a man treats me I can always tell whether he is in reality a gentleman or only a common man dressed in a gentleman's clothes. A man may lift his hat to a lady in passing her upon the street, and yet be at heart a most contemptible creature; but if he can lift his hat as

18

cordially and speak as politely to me, a poor
old colored man, as to a fine lady or a million-
aire, then I am sure he is, in whatever else he
may be wanting, a true gentleman. The most
perfect and beautiful gentleman I ever saw was
an officer in the Forty-ninth Massachusetts
Infantry. He was strong as an ox, a hard
fighter, and never knew fear. No soldier under
his command dared to disobey him, for he was
very strict; and yet all the men respected, and
most of them loved him, because he was kind
and considerate as well as brave and resolute.
He did not treat alike the common soldiers and
the under-officers, but he was equally polite to
all; and he never seemed to display his authority more than was necessary."

I cannot recall the precise words used by
"Old Jeff," but I believe I have reproduced
his ideas without changing any shade of meaning, and in phrases not wholly unlike his own.
He always described himself as uneducated,
and, judged by the rules of the schools, such
he certainly was; and yet he was not ill-informed with regard to matters of common and
ordinary interest, and he knew many things
one might search a long time without finding.
Henry Ward Beecher once said of education:

" It is the knowledge of how to use the whole of
one's self. Men are often like knives with many

blades; they know how to open one, and only one; all the rest are buried in the handle, and they are no better than they would have been if they had been made with but one blade. Many men use but one or two faculties out of the score with which they are endowed. A man is educated who knows how to make a tool of every faculty—how to open it, how to keep it sharp, and how to apply it to all practical purposes."

Thus measured, no man is wholly educated, for in all are some dormant and undeveloped faculties; and it may be found, upon investigation, that the illiterate college-janitor has discovered, and strengthened by use, some mental, or even moral, quality of which the erudite college-president has not so much as dreamed. Judged by Mr. Beecher's standard, "Old Jeff" was not entirely uneducated, for he certainly knew how to make very good use of some of his mental faculties; and, if usefulness be a correct test of moral worth, he was more than educated—he was in the best sense a good man.

CLEAR SPIRITUAL ATMOSPHERE

NIHIL est in intellectu, quod non fuerit in sensu, is the Latin for, "Let us eat and drink, for to-morrow we die." If the intellect is a beggar living upon the charity of the five senses, then let us be sure that there is neither God nor immortality, for never have we seen with mortal eye or touched with material hand the mighty Spirit that created all. If our Latin line be true we may add another, and it shall be equally true: *Post mortem nihil est, ipsaque mors nihil.* We are fooled and defrauded by a psychology of the pineal gland and nervous plexus, and are made to go, like the beast, face downward, with every hope and aspiration geocentric. The motto of this miserable psychology, if psychology of any kind it may be called, is well summed up in an old Neapolitan inscription over a tavern of which the Neapolitans themselves were ashamed:

> "Amici, alliegre magnammo e bevimmo
> Fin che n' ci stace uoglio e la lucerna :
> Chi sa s'a l'autro munno n' ci vedimmo ?
> Chi sa s'a l'autro munno n' c' è taverna ?"

Certain materialistic philosophers are enquiring: "Is this the best of possible worlds?" Perhaps not! The gourmand who fails of obtaining all the terrapin and champagne he desires has a ground of complaint. He who wants a sovereign and has only a shilling is not without a grievance. But the fact that God made this world to His own mind satisfies me, and I can see that His glory is better than the beastly gratification of the *bon vivant*. I admire the magnanimity of spirit that prompts certain atheists to surrender, without hope of future reward, all present pleasure and gain for the good of their fellow-men; but I experience only nausea and disgust when I contemplate the self-complacent unbelief of the well-fed literary coxcomb, who, because he chances to have all the champagne and ortolan he can stuff into his gastric-sac, finds it impossible to see how any one can expect or wish for an immortality which appears to him only another squeezed lemon. There is an atheism of the head, which is not infrequently associated with noble thinking and useful living; there is an atheism of the heart, which springs from and results in moral corruption; and there is an atheism of the digestive organs, which having said to the belly, "Thou art my god," finds its holiest aspirations more than realized in a luxuriously selfish life.

The lower the personal experience, the more hopeless the creed evolved. At last the man, reduced to the level of an oyster, so far as any semblance of moral spine is concerned, entertains only such convictions as might adorn the pulp of a bivalve. Mud and slime may be good for the oyster, but without sunshine and blue sky there can be no high thinking, noble aspiration, and inspiring romance. Better than the swamp-gas of materialism is the too thin air of mysticism. Dionysius the Areopagite has had a large family of dreamers, but there have been among them many sons and daughters of power and enchantment. Hegel is there with his *Methode der Absoluten Negativiat*. There also may be found Angelus Silesius, who was a good man for all his *Ich bin so gross als Gott*. In that great company is old Jacob Behmen of the *Dialogues on the Supersensual Life*. These are strange men, but they do not crush us into the earth. They lift us into an atmosphere so high as to be almost irrespirable, but we have the sunshine and the blue sky. And with clear spiritual atmosphere comes freedom from anthropomorphic restraints (so far as such freedom is possible to the human mind) and conventional subserviency to smug definitions. We are lifted out from the ooze and mud and are introduced into the sunshine. The low rafters

disappear and the azure heavens are our roof.
Heraclitus may be right when he teaches that
"the god who owns the oracle of the Delphian
Apollo neither reveals nor conceals, but intimates, σημαίνει, signifies by sign or symbol;" but the God of heaven and earth makes
a temple of the soul that will receive Him.
Near acquaintance renders diaphanous the
symbol. They who realize the Divine Presence
care little for definitions. Joubert said, "We
know God easily provided we do not constrain
ourselves to define Him." In formulating the
Deity we construct Him in our own image.
He is a concept, and as such must resemble
the mind that gives Him form. We worship
the God we have created, and not the God
who created us; and it is hard to see how in
the matter of idolatry we have any advantage
over our friends across the sea who openly
adore the work of their own hands. Better
than any image of God, conceived by the mind
or graven by the hand, is the quiet conscious-
ness of His presence and love. What Faust
says to Margaret, when she doubts if he believes in God, is in place here:

" Who dares to name him?
And who dares to acknowledge:
' I believe him? '

Who can feel,
And presume
To say, ' I believe not in him? '
The One who embraces all,
The Preserver of all.''

STAGE-FRIGHT

THE announcement in the *Albany Evening Journal* of March 8, 1899, of the death from stage-fright of Mrs. Dennis Tabor, opens up a large field of speculation and investigation. Mrs. Tabor had charge of a meeting of the Woman's Christian Temperance Union in the Baptist Church at Hilton, N. Y., and was reading aloud the Scripture lesson when a sudden paroxysm of fear overcame her, rendering her unconscious; in which state she remained a few hours, and then died.

The distressing death of this good woman while leading her associates in public worship reminds me of a book written by a distinguished Frenchman, M. Gélineau, on *Phobiæ*, in which is given a complete list of the various kinds of unearthly fear known to the student of mental science. There is no occasion for burdening the reader's memory with an unabridged transcript, but here are a few of the horrors that assail human imagination:

1. Aichmophobia, or fear of sharp points, as of needles.

2. Agaraphobia, or fear of open spaces (with subvarieties, as Thalassophobia, or dread of the ocean, and Astrophobia, or fear of the stars and celestial spaces).

3. Mysophobia, or fear of filth.

4. Hæmatophobia, or dread of blood.

5. Necrophobia, or horror of dead bodies.

6. Thanatophobia, or dread of death.

7. Monophobia, or fear of solitude.

8. Bacillophobia, or fear of microbes.

9. Pathophobia, or fear of disease (with many subdivisions, one of the most important of which is Zoöphobia, or fear of animals, which in its turn has subdivisions for cats, dogs, horses, mice, etc., *ad totum catalogium animalium*).

10. Kleptophobia, or fear of becoming a kleptomaniac.

11. Pyrophobia, or fear of matches.

12. Stasophobia, or fear of evil results from standing upright.

13. Acrophobia, or fear of high places.

14. Demonophobia, or dread of the devil.

15. Phobophobia, or fear of having fear.

M. Gélineau has also a bewildering list of phobiæ peculiar to the members of various professions. Ministers, physicians, lawyers, actors, artists, teachers, authors, and editors stand upon the very pinnacle of peril, and are liable to be at any moment transfixed by the deadly shaft of

fear. These phobiæ are not all of them Hellen-
ized, but they are described with grim minute-
ness of detail, and one who reads the list does
so in the face of a moral certainty that he himself will be counted among the slain. The old
lady who listened to a lecture on " The Circula-
tion of the Blood " returned home in extreme
depression of spirit, declaring that the circula-
tion of the blood was the one thing she had
dreaded all her life, and that now she knew she
had it in one of its most aggravated forms.
One has only to read M. Gélineau's book to
know by personal experience what are the internal and infernal horrors of which the work
treats. There is a wonderful contagion in fear,
as every soldier knows who has participated in
a military retreat—a contagion both blinding
and persistent. General Grant, in his *Reminiscences*, says:

" I once saw as many as four or five thousand
stragglers lying under cover of the river bluff,
panic-stricken, most of whom would have been
shot where they lay, without resistance, before they
would have taken muskets and marched to the
front to protect themselves. I heard General Buell
berating them and trying to shame them into join-
ing their regiments. He even threatened them
with shells from the gunboats near by. But it was
all to no effect. Most of these men afterwards

proved themselves as gallant as any of those who saved the battle from which they had deserted."

Panic is truly the echo of Pan's wild voice, only the ancient deity has forsaken the silvan retreats and classic shepherds to hide in the thick jungles of bewildered minds. The song of the Sirens was death, but I doubt if the cry of Pan is much to be preferred. There have been cases in which men have come suddenly under the power of uncontrollable fear without being able to discover any cause. A prominent actor who had been before the public more than twenty years was so paralyzed by stage-fright that he lost his voice. The morning papers said that soon after the play commenced he was disabled by an attack of aphony, but he later confessed to some of his friends the true secret of his discomfiture. He never fully regained his confidence, and was glad when an opportunity presented of retiring from professional life. I am well acquainted with a clergyman who, though he knows by heart the Lord's Prayer and the Ten Commandments, cannot repeat either of them in public without having before him the printed page. I know another clergyman who has so firmly fixed in his mind a fear that he could not read the Twenty-third Psalm from the pulpit that nothing could induce him to make the attempt. Once I was in a pulpit, at a missionary convention, when a clergyman who sat by my side turned to me and said, " I should be very grateful if you would read the Scripture lesson that has been assigned me." After I had read the lesson I enquired if he were ill. " No," said he, " I am not ill, but I had a feeling that it would be impossible for me to read aloud the chapter selected for me ; and so strong was the feeling that I had not the courage to stand up and open the Bible." Later the clergyman rose and with perfect self-composure made the most eloquent address that was delivered that evening.

An English journal relates the following amusing and painful anecdote of the late Mr. James Johnston, who was once a member of Parliament :

" On his first taking his seat in the House he was said to have framed a ' maiden ' speech, in the course of which he expected to rival Demosthenes; but it so happened that, though the speech was transferred from his head to the lining of his hat, yet the perspicuity of utterance fled. He rose, essayed to speak, but in vain ; and he reseated himself in silent dismay, without articulating a word. The members of the Eccentrics' Club, of which Mark Supple was the Chairman, taking advantage of this unfortunate failure, caused papers to be printed, and circulated, and, as was then the fashion in London, cried through the streets of Westminster and the city, on the top of which appeared in large type, 'THE MAIDEN SPEECH OF JAMES JOHNSTON, ESQ., M. P. FOR SANDWICH, AS DELIVERED, YESTERDAY IN PARLIAMENT.' The rest of the paper was blank. The wife of the honorable gentleman heard the outcry as she sat at her window in Great George Street, and exulting in the consequence and popularity of her husband, instantly called for her footman, and desired he would purchase some of the papers of the poor man in the street. He having obeyed her commands, immediately presented them to the lady, who, on viewing the blank paper, exclaimed with great violence. 'Why, Richard, you are a fool; you have brought nothing!' 'No, my lady,' dryly replied the servant, 'it is my master, for he said nothing.' "

A highly cultivated man whose conversation was a delight, and whose mind was stored with the wealth of thirty years of scholarly reading and thinking, said: " I do not understand the self-confidence that enables one to preach or act in a play with no tremor of the nerves. I could not utter five words in the presence of an audience though I am quite able to hold my own in the parlor or at the club." Hawthorne was drenched in a cold perspiration at the thought of a public dinner. It is said of Wendell Phillips that he never began a speech or lecture without 'stage-fright.' George Vandenhoff, in his *Leaves from an Actor's Note-Book*, records with some surprise that he was not in the least nervous when he stepped out before the foot-lights for the first time. He thinks his coolness was the result of inexperience, because he never again had such perfect self-possession. Later in his professional career when he had won his laurels, he was thankful if he could say, " I am tolerably calm." He says:

"I confess I was not overwhelmed with terror at appearing before the much dreaded tribunal of a London audience, though it was my first essay in arms, and much depended on the result. I made, I remember, a very hearty dinner about three o'clock, went calmly down to the Theatre at six, dressed, and 'made up' my face in quite a business-like manner, (I wore, by the bye, for my first dress the very same costume that John Kemble had worn for the part; think of that for a novice! 'Shade of Kemble,' I internally exclaimed, 'let thy mantle fall on me!') and entered the Green Room cool and self-possessed. There was Charles Mathews, dressed for Michael Perez, and also Madame Vestris. On my replying to their inquiries that I felt perfectly at ease, Mathews, placing his hand on my left breast, said—'Let 's see; let 's feel!' He kept his hand there a moment, then withdrawing it, exclaimed to Vestris,—'By Jove, Liz, it's as calm as a child's!' 'Now then,' said I, 'let me feel how *yours* goes.' 'Oh no!' said he, 'I'm as nervous as I can be!'"

After fifty years of great acting Farren approached the "first nights" of a new play with trembling and the gravest apprehension. On one occasion, in the "Irish Heiress," he was so overcome by "stage-fright" that he could not remember his part, and had to be prompted through an entire scene. Macready often approached the stage as a culprit goes to the gallows. When the curtain rose the cold sweat stood in beads upon his forehead.

Major J. B. Pond wrote some time ago, in the *Cosmopolitan*, this about his friend John B. Gough:

"It is strange, but it is a fact, that although Gough never broke down in his life as an orator, and never failed to capture his audience, he always had a mild sort of stage-fright which never vanished until he began to speak. To get time to master this fright was his reason for insisting upon being "introduced" to his audiences before he spoke, and he so insisted even in New England, where the absurd custom had been abandoned for years. While the chairman was introducing him, Mr. Gough was "bracing up" to overcome his stage-fright. By the way, let me say right here (as the phrase "bracing up" has two meanings) that the slanderous statements often started against Mr. Gough, to the effect that he sometimes took a drink in secret, were wholly and wickedly untrue. In his autobiography Mr. Gough has told the story of his fall, his conversion, and his one relapse, and has told it truthfully. He was absolutely and always, after his first relapse, a total abstinence man in creed and life. There never lived a truer man."

An officer in the Sixth Presbyterian Church of Albany told me of a clergyman known to him, who, having resolved to try preaching without notes, went to a strange church in exchange with its pastor, and left his written sermon at home. He conducted the service without embarrassment, but, after announcing the text, found himself unable to utter a single word of his sermon though its theme had been carefully studied and much of its material memorized. He lost entire control of himself, and fled from the church as fast as his legs could carry him.

Even an experienced and trained speaker may be overcome by stage-fright in the very moment when he most counts upon success.

"The felicitous and facetious Jeffrey rose to present John Philip Kemble with a gold snuff-box at

17

a public dinner in Edinburgh. He rose with full confidence in that extemporaneous power which had never failed him, but when the dramatist raised his kingly form at the same instant and confronted the diminutive man with his magnificent obeisance —the grandest, probably, ever made by mortal— the most fluent of speakers was suddenly struck dumb. He sat down, with his speech unfinished and the golden gift unpresented."

It is recorded of Dr. Westfield, the Bishop of Bristol in the reign of Charles I., that he never entered the pulpit, even when he had been fifty years a preacher, without trembling. Upon one occasion when preaching before the king at Oxford, he was so overcome by "stage-fright" that he fainted away. His Majesty waited patiently for the good man's recovery, and then had from him a sermon of rare power and eloquence.

It is related that when President McKinley arrived at Buffalo to visit the Pan-American Exposition which was held in that city in 1901, he enquired of Mr. Scatcherd, who was upon the Committee of Reception, "When am I to make my speech?" Mr. Scatcherd replied, "Early to-morrow forenoon." "Well," said the President, "I am glad of that: I'll not be able to have any fun until I have got my speech off my mind." "Public speaking should not cause you any nervous apprehension," responded Mr. Scatcherd, "you 've been at it so long." "Well it does," said the President; "I am just as nervous before a speech in these days as I was before my maiden address in the House of Representatives years and years ago."

The editor of an Albany paper, commenting upon President McKinley's nervous apprehensions, added these lines that are true in every word, as all public speakers who have influenced the minds of men can easily understand.

"The man who is so stolid that he knows no nervousness, fear, or timidity, is certainly not fit for oratory, or for generalship, and, indeed, upon the spur of the moment, one can hardly think of any calling in life in which such a man would shine. It is the man whose nerves are keenly alive and all a-quiver—yet under the control of his mind and will—who makes a stir in the world of thought and action."

THE RESOURCES OF NATURE

THE naturalist Karl Piotz has given the
scientific world thirty volumes, most of
which treat of butterflies; and in these are more
than ten thousand illustrations from his own
pencil. Karl Piotz's labors show how vast are
the resources of nature. Think of the countless
millions of tiny creatures that float in the air
and bask in the sunbeam. There are collections that contain seventy thousand distinct
species, and new varieties are constantly coming to the knowledge of scientific men. Every
drop of water, every grain of sand, every
breath of air is crowded with living creatures;
and we ourselves are walking zoölogical gar-
dens bearing about in our tissues trillions of
animalculæ. Both microscope and telescope
open for us the doors of infinity, and disclose
world within world, and world upon world. A
particle of dust floats through the open window
and falls upon my desk. I can brush it away
with my hand, or waft it into the air with my
breath, and yet it is a microcosm having laws

and a destiny of its own.   In the last analysis
the deepest ocean, and the highest mountain,
and indeed "the great globe itself," are but
vast collections of atoms or electrons.   You
may study and examine in any direction, and
never come to a boundary.   Upon all sides
shoreless possibilities invite and challenge the
mind of man.   Is there discouragement in this?
Is there not rather an exquisite delight, thrill-
ing the soul and rousing it to renewed activity?
If the universe is shoreless, we are qualified to
navigate its expanse; and if no harbor lies
before us, no storm may engulf our bark.
The introverted vision discovers the world of
thought to be as vast as the material universe
—indeed, the problems of mind are far more
wonderful than those of body.   In all this
there is an exhilaration that lifts from off us
the low roof of conventional thinking and
acting, and allows the wind of eternity to
blow in upon us with free and joyous wing.
The roof must be replaced with one more
exalted, and giving larger space for growth.
That in time must disappear to make room for
still another.   And ever as we outgrow ourselves, we sing:

" Build thee more stately mansions, O my soul,
    As the swift seasons roll !

Leave thy low-vaulted past !
Let each new temple, nobler than the last,
Shut thee from heaven with a dome more vast,
    Till thou at length art free,
Leaving thine outgrown shell by life's unresting
    sea ! "

BISMARCK'S CONTEMPT FOR THE PARISIANS

BISMARCK condensed the history of the French Revolution, so far as it concèrns Paris, to a single sentence not easily forgotten, when he said: "Take from the average native Parisian the tailor, the hairdresser, and the cook, what is left is Red Indian." Under all the fantastic refinements of the gay capital is a cruel ferocity more dreadful than that of the tiger. The wild savage of North American forests is a tender-hearted Christian gentleman when compared with the *sans-culottes*. I had much rather face a Sioux tomahawk than a red republican pike. Hegel was not mistaken when he affirmed that there was in all the French language no equivalent for the German *Gemüthlichkeit*. The red wine of lust is everywhere "on tap" in the city that could worship as a "Goddess of Reason" an almost naked courtesan, but you must go elsewhere for a refreshing draught of the milk of human kindness. He was a witty but not altogether

undiscerning physician who wrote: " The people of Paris may be divided into three classes:
those who have had syphilis, those who are
having it now, and those who will have it later
on." Yet, notwithstanding Bismarck's contempt for France, which was, as has been said,
not wholly unjust, and the caustic classification just quoted, I think Berlin may have
some reason for shame and humiliation. The
greatest venereal clinics of the world (those of
Casper, Posnet, Nitze, Frank, Lewin, Lesser,
Joseph, Hoffmann, Lassar, Wossidlo, Mitscher-
lich, Buschke, Behrend, Bruns, Heller, and
Brüning) are in that city; and it has been
facetiously said that the constantly increasing
supply of material—" *embarras de richesse* "—
for those much-needed but shameful clinics is
in direct connection with the increasing gayety
of the German capital.

RIDDLES AND ENIGMAS

THAT our riddles are degenerating into mere *jeux d'esprit* is a great calamity. When the solemn questions of life and destiny are changed into idle conceits, of what consequence can it be how they are answered? The fatal riddle of the Sphinx was no matter of wit and laughter. The strange question: "What being has four feet, two feet, and three feet; only one voice; but whose feet vary, and when it has most, is weakest?" so moved the men of Thebes that they gave Œdipus their kingdom and the hand of the queen for answering, "Man!" It required *oideo-pous*, swollen feet, to explain a riddle of the feet, and a man under the pressure of necessity to solve the problem of mankind. The fable relates that when the Sphinx found her occupation gone she leaped from a high rock; but she certainly did not destroy herself, for the poet's lines are still true:

> "The Sphinx is drowsy,
> Her wings are furled;
> Her ear is heavy,
> She broods on the world."

She will continue to "brood on the world," every moment demanding "the fate of the man-child and the meaning of man." They who solve the riddle of their own humanity save themselves and others, while all who fail are devoured. It was no shrewd guess on the part of Œdipus—he was the answer, and in self-recognition he solved the problem. It took the right man, but the moment of necessity was needed to bring him out. That moment, so fatal to all the fools in Thebes, was the coronation of Œdipus. For nothing should a wise man return deeper thanks than for necessity. It brings him in contact with himself, disciplines his affections, ripens his understanding, strengthens his nature, and enriches his experience; it thrusts goodness and greatness upon him—it does more, it reveals to him the goodness and greatness latent in his nature. A moment of necessity is worth an age of opportunity. Ohnesargen's *Sphinx* in six volumes shows us how the riddle is fallen from its high place. A riddle is now only a conundrum, and often a very coarse one at that. The *Démande Joyeuse,* the treatise of the Abbé Cotiro, whose modesty did not prevent him from assuming the title *Le Père de l'Énigme* and the *Mercure de France*, all bear witness to the degradation of the riddle.

Samson's riddle is personal and comes nearer to our idea of an enigma, but the men of his time were deeply exercised over its solution.

"Samson said, 'Out of the eater came forth meat, and out of the strong came forth sweetness.' And they could not in three days expound the riddle. And it came to pass on the seventh day, that they said unto Samson's wife, 'Entice thy husband, that he may declare unto us the riddle, lest we burn thee and thy father's house with fire.' And Samson's wife wept before him and said, 'Thou dost but hate me, and lovest me not: thou hast put forth a riddle unto the children of my people and hast not told it me.' And he said unto her, 'Behold, I have not told it my father nor my mother, and shall I tell it thee?' And she wept before him the seven days, while their feast lasted; and it came to pass on the seventh day that he told her, because she lay sore upon him; and she told the riddle to the children of her people. And the men of the city said unto him on the seventh day before the sun went down, 'What is sweeter than honey? and what is stronger than a lion?' And he said unto them, 'If ye had not ploughed with my heifer, ye had not found out my riddle.'"—Judges xiv., 14–18.

The riddle was one of rare ingenuity, and in the original could be turned in every conceivable direction without disclosing its true

meaning. It was clear as glass, and yet so ob-
scure that the Philistines utterly failed to solve it
until they ploughed with Samson's heifer. The
riddle has a curious parallel in the German story
of a woman who interceded for her husband.
The man was under sentence of death, but the
judges promised to release him if his wife
would give them a riddle the meaning of
which they could not make out. The woman
remembered that she had that day passed a
dead horse by the roadside, and that between
its ribs was a bird's nest containing six young
birds, which she took with her. She therefore
propounded this riddle:

" As ik hin güng, as ik wedder kam,
    Den Lebendigen ik uet den Doden nam.
Süss (Sechs) de güngen de Saewten (den Sie-
        benten) quitt,
    Raet to, gy Herren, nu ist Tyt."

The judges had no heifer with which to plough,
and so the culprit was released.

Some of Solomon's Proverbs are, strictly
speaking, riddles. Josephus describes a contest in riddles, in which Solomon vanquished
Hiram, King of Tyre, and was himself defeated
by one of Hiram's subjects. An English writer
calls it a philosophical gambling match. Large
sums of money were lost and won at ancient

riddle-matches. The "hard questions" with which the Queen of Sheba proved Solomon are believed to have been riddles. Erasmus thinks our Saviour employed the riddle in Matthew xii., 43–45. We have a riddle in Revelation xiii., 16, and a challenge to its solution in the eighteenth verse. The Syrinx of Theocritus is a famous example of the classic enigma. Homer's death is said to have been caused by mortification at not being able to solve a riddle. The most inexplicable of all riddles is called, from a Latin inscription at Bologna, "Ælia Lælia Crispis," and may be translated into English thus:

ÆLIA LÆLIA CRISPIS.

"Neither man, nor woman, nor androgyne ;
Neither girl, nor boy, nor eld ;
Neither harlot, nor virgin ;
   But all (of these).

Carried off neither by hunger, nor sword, nor
   poison ;
   But by all (of them).
Neither in heaven, nor in the water, nor in the
   earth ;
   But biding everywhere.

LUCIUS AGATHO PRISCUS.

"Neither the husband, nor lover, nor friend;
Neither grieving, nor rejoicing, nor weeping;
   But all (of these)—

This—neither a pile, nor a pyramid, nor a sepulchre
That is built, he knows and knows not (which it is).
It is a sepulchre containing no corpse within it;
It is a corpse with no sepulchre containing it;
  But the corpse and the sepulchre are one and the
    same."

Translated by E. Cobham Brewer.

Oriental riddles are mostly in the form of poetry; even the impromptu " cup-question," given out at a festival or banquet, must be in verse. When the riddle is published the author appends the answer " up-side-down." Here are two illustrations from Hariri, elegantly translated by Rev. William R. Alger:

  " It is a more prodigious tree.
  A weaker man it seems to be.
  It is its fate to join with all
  The solid things upon this ball.
  But with the falling of its foe,—
  How strange it is!—itself doth go."

" When the sun flies,
The *shadow* dies."

" What dried-up stick, before or since the flood,
Was turned into a thing of flesh and blood ? "

" His *staff* did Moses make
A live and crawling snake."

One of the best forms of the riddle is the anagram, specimens of which may be found in Hebrew literature. The ancient Jews ascribed to it cabalistic and occult qualities. Plato entertained curious superstitions with regard to it, and thought that every man's destiny might be discovered from his anagram. The solemn Puritans employed it in sermons and hymns, and for political purposes. Thus Cotton Mather, extolling the virtues of John Wilson, the first pastor in Boston, speaks of

" His care to guide his flock and feed his lambs
  By words, works, prayers, psalms, alms, and
    anagrams."

Camden has devoted considerable space in his *Remains* to the subject of anagrams, and a very pleasing chapter on both anagrams and echo-verses may be found in Disraeli's *Curiosities of Literature*. The best of all anagrams is that which changes Pilate's question to our Saviour —*Quid est veritas?*—into the only true answer, *Est vir qui adest*. The author of the famous anagram is unknown, but he was certainly a very devout and skilful artist in words. Some of the most ingenious and interesting of the many anagrams on record are :—Charles James Stuart (" Pretender "), claims Arthur's Seat; Marie

Touchet (mistress of Charles IX.), *Je charme tout;* Frère Jaques Clement (assassin of Henry III.), *C'est l'enfer qui m'a créé;* Georgius Monke, Dux de Aumarle, *Ego regem reduxi Ano. Sa. MDCLVV;* Sir Roger Charles Doughty Tichborne, Baronet, You horrid butcher, Orton, biggest rascal here; Horatio Nelson, *Honor est a Nilo.* Lady Eleanor Davies, wife of the poet Sir John Davies, thought herself a prophetess, because she found in her name the anagram " Reveal, O Daniel!" She published a number of mad predictions of questionable patriotism which brought down upon her the vengeance of the authorities. The discovery of the following anagram robbed the good lady of her dear delusion—" Dame Eleanor Davies, never so mad a ladie!" It was a better anagram than the first, which had an *L* that did not belong to it, and was wanting by an *S.* Frenzelius, an eccentric German, boasted that for fifty years he had kept up the practice of celebrating, by way of obituary, the names of distinguished persons "called down into the grave," and that in every case he had produced a successful anagram. He tells us that the cheerful occupation was attended with physical torments resembling the death-pangs of the persons whose names he anagrammatized.

The modern riddle is generally a puzzle—

sometimes it is little more than a coarse jest.
Having no object in view but that of amusement, it is so arranged as to provoke laughter.
Here is a specimen from the sixteenth century—
riddles have not improved since then: "What
is the worst bestowed charity that one can
give? Alms to a blind man; for he would be glad
to *see* the person hanged that gave it to him."
Here is a riddle in the form of a conundrum and
bearing evidence of very recent construction:
"Why is this insurance policy a contradictory
thing? Because when I can't sell it I can-cel
it; and when I can-cel it I can't sell it." Schil-
ler sought to restore the riddle to its original
religious solemnity, and he succeeded so far as
to invest it with a certain literary finish, but
no farther. Dr. Oliver Wendell Holmes has
given us one of the most ingenious of rhymed
riddles:

> "'I'm going to blank,' with failing breath,
>   The falling gladiator said;
> Unconquered, he 'consents to death;'
>   One gasp—the hero soul has fled.
> 'I'm going to blank,' the school-boy cried;
>   Two sugared sweets his hands display—
> Like snow-flakes in the ocean tide
>   They vanish, melted both away.
> Tell with one verb, or I'll tell you,
> What each was just about to do."

19

From a dozen answers to the above we select
two :

"'Succumb,' the gladiator groans,
  And breathes away his life with moans;
  'Suck 'em,' the school-boy cries in glee—
  You need n't, Dr. Holmes, tell me—SUCKER."

" This blank blank verse is well, no doubt,
    Although it breathes a Holmesic strain;
  But certain facts have been left out,
    Which mark this interesting twain.
  Obedient to some mystic plan,
    Like language still their lips employ—
  'I 'm gladiator,' sighs the man,
    'I 'm glad I ate 'em,' cries the boy.
  And he whom mortal thrust hath pricked
    Quite fails his rival to outdo,
  For while he owns he 's badly licked,
    The school-boy boasts that he 's licked two."

CHIPS FROM A LITERARY
WORKSHOP

INTROSPECTION

I QUESTION the propriety of spending much time in early life over introspective studies. We need a firm grasp upon surrounding realities before we put to ourselves the riddle of the Sphinx, which we shall find no matter of wit and laughter. The fable is at fault that tells us the Sphinx, when she found her perplexing question answered, leaped to her death. She continues to "brood on the world," every moment demanding "the fate of the man-child and the meaning of man." They who would solve this riddle of their own humanity must first know much of the surrounding universe. It was by no shrewd guess that Œdipus won the crown from all the fools in Thebes. Behind the answer "Man" was a man's clear perception of himself as he stood out in bold relief against an objective background. To start questions one cannot answer is to unsettle the mind, destroy the foundations of conviction, and establish a habit of insincerity. Too much introspection has made many a sceptic and paralyzed many a noble will. It is the old story of the perplexed centipede :

> " The centipede was happy quite,
>   Until the toad for fun
> Said, ' Pray which leg comes after which ? '
> This worked her mind to such a pitch
> She lay distracted in a ditch
>   Considering how to run. "

REMORSE

"Away with remorse !" cries Lamettrie, the gay and brilliant author of *l'Histoire Naturelle de l'Ame*, " it is a weakness, an outcome of education." What a pity it is Lamettrie was not near to comfort Judas Iscariot, the Emperor Nero, Charles IX. of France, and Benedict Arnold, when those great men were ruthlessly crushed beneath the iron heel of that " outcome of education." With what enchanting grace and ease the hand that penned *l'Homme-machine* waves away all the self-reproach and self-revenge that made a monarch's blood to ooze through the pores of his skin, and to start from the corners of his eyes and from his nostrils. Could that monarch only have known that all his self-accusations were but " weakness and the outcome of education," great would have been his peace of mind, even when forced to contemplate the Massacre of St. Bartholomew's Day. Poor Judas!—his death was entirely due to over-education.

CELLINI'S DREAM

Benvenuto Cellini, after a terrible dream which he had in the castle of St. Angelo, saw a light over his head wherever he went, and though the flame burned with greater brightness when the grass was wet with dew, it never entirely disappeared. The human soul, like the great sculptor, often beholds, after some dreadful calamity, a luminous presence and sees with clearer vision. Troubles, like thunder-storms, purify the atmosphere, and when the sun shines out upon the moist sod, glistening with crystal beauty, the soul discovers new grace and larger truth on every side. In a shower of tears God often sets the rainbow of His promise.

COURTESY

He was doubtless an honest alderman, but he was not quite up to Chesterfield's ideal of a fine gentleman, who, delighted by the appetite of Prince William of Gloucester at a public banquet, cried out, "Eat away, your royal high ness; there 's aplenty more in the kitchen." But men and things are good or bad, fine or coarse by comparison; and it seems to us that the Liverpool alderman was even squeamishly delicate in his choice of phrases, when we find one western governor telling the United States authorities to "shut up," and another replying to his critics after the following fashion: "Let them pitch in and give me the devil if they want to. They could not cut through my hide in three weeks with an axe." A little of the politeness and courtesy of older nations might not hurt the robust constitution of our American Republic.

GENTLEMAN AND LADY

A gentleman is such at heart or he is no gentleman at all. A woman may have every grace and refinement, may be able to enter and leave a room with faultless ease and dignity, may have a delicate acquaintance with all the niceties of the French language, may be able to say pleasing things in a captivating way, may be well qualified to shine in gay society, and yet be no lady in the true sense of that word. It requires more than mere polish to make either gentleman or lady. One might have rough hands, hardened by honest toil, a spinal column bent double from long familiarity with drudgery, an awkward shyness, and a good-natured yet distressing bluntness —might have all these and yet merit the name of gentleman or lady. It was of our blessed Lord and Saviour that the quaint old Thomas Dekker wrote these lines:

> " The best of men
> That e'er wore earth about him was a sufferer ;
> A soft, meek, patient, humble, tranquil spirit,
> The first true gentleman that ever breathed."

ENGLISH SELF-ASSERTION

The vulgar self-assertion of the average Englishman may be extremely disagreeable, but it underlies and is the foundation of a large part of British greatness. Self-confidence is the first and most important step in the direction of all conquest. It may be true that England's day of proud supremacy has passed away forever, but it is also true that so long as the English people retain their firm and deep-seated belief in themselves, so long will there be vitality in English institutions and courage in British hearts.

TASTE FOR SCANDAL

The taste for scandal is said to be characteristic of the American people, but it is doubtful whether the charge can be sustained. Americans, it is true, are fond of excitement and given to the pleasures of curiosity. But curiosity and the love of scandal are not the same thing. Curiosity is characteristic of the child, while love of scandal dwells in minds somewhat *blasé* —minds that have grown old in scenes of intrigue and debauchery. Curiosity and innocence often go hand in hand; but for the love of scandal innocence has no friendliness. The rustic is given to curiosity, the courtier to scandal-making. America is an infant nation; eager, curious, active, and inventive. It has young blood in its veins and the fire of energy in its nerves. When it has grown old it may, like other nations, sip poisoned honey from stained and faded flowers; but at present it is, like its great rivers and rolling prairies, fresh and pure.

Scandal, like a rank weed, grows round the tottering columns of an old and weak government. It needs the soil of aristocracy, which is mostly muck. It cannot take root in the fresh and rocky ground of a new and living government. It needs courtiers, priests, lords, and the genial atmosphere of a corrupt throne.

WALTER PATER'S PHILOSOPHY

Walter Pater's style is delightful; his themes are rich and gloriously ornate with the splendor of Hellenic life, softened by the Italian Renaissance; but why must he have with it all a philoso-

phy so disheartening and distressing ? Is it the
mission of artistic and literary beauty to dis-
courage? Upon well-nigh every page is the
Cyrenaic shadow of that saddest of beliefs
which makes pleasure the great end of human
living. And it is not a wholesome and robust
pleasure such as befits a man of athletic frame
and noble parts; it is a melancholy delight that
dances like Jack-o'-Lantern over the grave of a
great hope. "Our one chance," writes Pater,
"lies in getting as many pulsations as possible
into the given time." Pulsations! Yes, but
one hears under and through all the ever-recur-
ring refrain, "To-morrow we die." Wilful
sadness is an evil thing, and not less evil is that
philosophy of pleasure which leads at last to
darkness and despair.

GENIUS A THING OF ITS OWN AGE.

William Blake wrote, "The ages are all equal,
but genius is always above its age." Let it be
conceded that genius is in advance of its age,
still it must not be forgotten that genius is also
of its age in every essential feature. It takes
color and form from circumstances and environ-
ment. Shakespeare, who created a world of
wisdom and beauty for all ages, was yet the
child of his own. He is known only as we study
him in the light of race, time, training, person-

ality, and much beside. All these he absorbed as the tree sucks up from the earth nutritious juices; and all these he has transmuted into those superb dramas that render his name immortal, even as the tree changes sap into delicious fruit. There is a sense in which genius transcends its age, but there is a more important, because more vital, sense, in which that genius is of the very fibre of the age from which it takes its rise and derives its growth, and in which forevermore it retains its root.

ARNOLD'S " EMPEDOCLES ON ETNA "

Arnold's " Empedocles on Etna " fails in this, that its mournful introspection is untrue to life. It is a poetical morass, full of mephitic vapors and " stagnant sadness," and its superb beauty draws all its illumination from decay. In it there is no motion of wind or wave. Its misery is so utterly devoid of real action that there is left no space for even the faintest hope of relief. There can be no leadership without hope. The poets of pessimism leave us where they find us, since they have for us and all the world no mission of helpfulness, and no word of uplifting. From the beginning of time the leaders of men have been optimists. Even Tolstoi, with his terrible disclosures of the distress and oppression of man's lot on earth, heart-breaking as he is at times, still inspires to resistance and encourages to hope. Better one day with Chaucer than a thousand years in " The City of Dreadful Night."

DIOGENES' TUB

Diogenes was as proud of his tub as was Alexander of his throne; and as between tub and throne, the latter was the better because it represented larger opportunity of service and a richer and nobler culture. The man who is satisfied with little or nothing is of no great value to the world.   I see in the tub neither modesty nor humility, but unworthy pride in a poor thing. Alexander's offer was kind and generous, and merited consideration from Diogenes. There is just as pitiful and paltry a vanity beneath the tub-like costume of the Quaker as may be found under the throne-like vestments of the Roman Catholic Cardinal.

THE SAVAGE SURVIVES IN EVERY MAN

" I want free life, and I want fresh air ;
　And I sigh for the canter after the cattle,
　The *mêlée* of horns and hoofs and heads
　That wars and wrangles and scatters and
　　　spreads ;
　The green beneath and the blue above,
　And dash and danger, and life and love,
　And Lasca ! "

There is in every man a something that persists and asserts itself through all the toning-down processes of civilization. As the shell is supposed to sing of the distant sea whence it was taken, so this something in man forever suggests the original humanity of free life and fresh air for which the poet sighs. The savage is never wholly eradicated, but survives the fine pruning and dressing of culture, to come exuberantly to the surface when least expected, full of primitive and self-assertive force. We are never so far away from the early progenitor as sometimes appears; and it is doubtful if, with all our intellectual and social training, we ever succeed in wholly cutting his acquaintance. There is precisely the same substratum of human nature in Matthew Arnold that we have in Spotted-Tail ; and, in spite of the most stringent conventionality, every man at times longs for

> " The green beneath and the blue above,
>   And dash and danger, and life and love,
>   And Lasca ! "

TRUE COURAGE

Turenne displayed true courage when in the hour of battle he thus addressed himself: "You are trembling, carcass of mine; you would tremble more could you know where I am going to take you." He was alive to the actual danger by which he was surrounded, and yet unshaken in his resolve to face without flinching every peril it was his duty to encounter. Unknown and uncomprehended dangers may be met in a reckless spirit; only those evils which we see and understand admit of true bravery in the way in which we deal with them. Where there is no fear there can be no courage. He only who still desires to live can die the death of a brave man. The religious enthusiast who, despising this world and longing for a better, courts martyrdom, is no hero at all when compared with the soldier who resolutely exposes himself to a death of indescribable agony from which every nerve in his body shrinks, and from which his whole soul recoils. Pale cheeks, bloodless lips, and trembling knees are not signs of cowardice when the soul remains dauntless. Jesus was not less a hero for that cry in the garden, "O my Father, if it be possible, let this cup pass from me"—not less a hero because the cry was followed by the stern resolve of duty, "Nevertheless, not as I will, but as Thou wilt."

THE GREAT ECCLESIASTICAL LIE

To me, a Protestant, there can be no confessional but the closet of prayer, and no priest but the crucified, risen, and ascended Christ. God forbid that I should call any man, whether in Roman or Anglican orders, priest. May I never in any hour of weakness so far forget the One to whom alone I am responsible for all my conduct, as to imagine that a sinful man like myself can have any power whatever to absolve the soul from either sin or its dreadful consequences. May the great ecclesiastical lie of the centuries, that God has given His honor to another, never cast its fatal shadow over my conscience.

THE MINISTRY OF NATURE

The ministry of Nature—what a priesthood and service! No gowned ecclesiastic, to the tinkling of silver bells and the dizzy blaze of superstitious lights, kneels at the altar of the hills. There, in silence, broken only by the songs of happy birds, descends the benediction of the Heavenly Father in sunlight and shadow upon the children of the Divine Love.

"KRAFT UND STOFF"

I have just finished reading Buchner's "Kraft und Stoff," and am sure I do the work no injustice in describing its gross materialism as—

A faith that grasps the outer shell,
  But never seeks for hidden fruit ;
And to explain the soul of song
  Would weigh and measure pipe and lute.

THE HISTORIC EPISCOPATE

The Lambeth Conference wants all Christians of every name and description to accept the historic episcopate, but they will never do anything of the kind. We are as anxious for both Christian and church union as are the members of the Lambeth Conference, but we distinguish between union and absorption. It seems to us that these Lambeth friends are hungering not so much for Christian union as for sectarian conquest; and that, deprived of ecclesiastical verbiage, their proposition is only a new rendering of the old nursery rhyme:

  " Walk into my parlor,
    Said the spider to the fly."

WHAT IS OBSOLETE MUST PERISH

The effort to retain an obsolete church, an effete government, or an antiquated superstition has always proved a failure, and is like a child's endeavor to retain a melting icicle by squeezing it in its little fist—the firmer the grasp the more speedy the departure. While a man repeats a dead creed with his lips, that very creed slips out of his heart and is gone. Liturgy is often only another way of spelling lethargy, and the creed from being a statement of belief too easily becomes a substitute for faith.

THE GOOD HERESY-HUNTER

The good heresy-hunter detects false doctrine a thousand miles away, and tracks it all around the globe. He goes a-gunning for ecclesiastical game, and his rifle is well loaded with the righteousness of Scribes and Pharisees.

TO DESERVE IS BETTER THAN TO SECURE

Pliny the elder wrote: "Always so act as to secure the love of your neighbor." The line were better written: "Always so act as to *deserve* the love of your neighbor." A greater than Pliny said: "Woe unto you when all men speak well of you."

ECCLESIASTICAL TOMFOOLERIES

Ecclesiastical tomfooleries have done more to discredit religion than all the unbelieving books this world has ever seen or is likely to see. Robert G. Ingersoll is a most devout and even superstitious defender of the faith when you compare him with the begowned gentlemen who exploit sacred tapestry, religious chandlery, and denominational trinkets.

IT IS EASIER TO APPEAR THAN TO BE

You may don Kant's old hat and wear it some time, if the custodians happen to be impecunious when you visit the museum; but to insinuate a few ounces of the philosopher's cerebrum under your own cap is quite another matter.

TIME SANCTIFIES

"Time sanctifies"—a list of ships may drop into Homer and become poetic; a catalogue of gods may creep into Juvenal and become artistic; a table of warriors may find its way into Virgil and lose all its commonplace dulness. A distinguished New England writer said: "Our reverence for the past is just in proportion to our ignorance of it." The statement is too strong, and yet the common proverb is drawn from ordinary experience, "Distance lends enchantment to the view." The halo of antiquity inspires awe, then veneration, and finally faith.

SACRED BOOKS ARE EXCLUSIVE

All sacred books are exclusive. They tolerate no rivals. The Kings do not indorse the Vedas; the Vedas cast out the Avesta; the Avesta leaves no place for the Koran; and the Bible, which we receive as the word of the only

20

living and true God, and which we rightly revere and love, refuses to share the honor of Divine authorship with any other work, ancient or modern. No book can be a holy Bible that is not also an only Bible.

CICERO AN UNCONSCIOUS HYPOCRITE

Cicero, with all his fine qualities, was still an unconscious hypocrite, deceiving himself as well as others; and his love for his country, the genuineness of which no one can doubt, was after all only a larger and more ambitious love for himself.

MAN WAS MADE TO BORROW

Polonius was mistaken when he advised, "Neither a borrower nor a lender be." Man was made to borrow. It is the sum of all human wisdom to borrow wisely and bravely. The "heir of all the ages" should make substantial drafts upon his patrimony.

EMERSON

When Whipple described Emerson as a "cross between Socrates and Sam Slick," he described the entire Yankee race, but he overlooked the good manners, inward as well as outward, that made the sage of Concord a representative of all that is best in every age and race.

DUTY BETTER THAN IMMORTALITY

" *Vetulam suam prætulit immortalitati,*"—
and so Ulysses chose the aged Penelope, when
Calypso would have given him herself and
immortality. The philosophy of that old
heathen is good for all ages and religions.
Better than immortality is duty well performed
in the face of every allurement. Live a loyal ·
and true life to-day, and thou hast truly lived,
even shouldst thou never live again.

TRUTHFULNESS

Even more important than the discovery of
truth is the cultivation of truthfulness. Thus
believed a good and beautiful thinker long
centuries ago:

Εἴ τίς με ἐλέγξαι, καὶ παραστῆσαί, μοι ὅτι οὐκ ὀρθῶς
ὑπολαμβάνω ἢ πράσσω, δύναται, χαίρων μεταθήσομαι·
ζητῶ γάρ τὴν ἀλήθειαν, ὑφ' ἧς οὐδεὶς πώποτε ἐβλάβη.
Βλάπτεται δὲ ὁ ἐπιμένων ἐπὶ τῆς ἑαυτοῦ ἀπάτης καὶ
ἀγνοίας·

CREED

After all it is possible to say against creeds
has been said, it still remains true that the
man is weak indeed and greatly to be pitied
who cannot say, " I believe."

STYLE

Professor Park tells us, in his *Memoir of Dr. Emmons*, that "style is only the frame to hold our thoughts. It is like the sash of a window ; a heavy sash will obstruct the light." Professor Park is astray. If what we say is important, how we say it is equally so. Style is not the opaque sash, but the transparent glass which, if it be without flaw and of right thickness, transmits unobstructed the pure light of thought. The value of an attractive style is best shown by the significant fact that he who decries it must do so in the very style he decries or go without readers.

DISTINCTIONS THAT RETARD THE FINAL CATASTROPHE

" Deepens now a grave,
Where every king and every slave
Shall drop his crown and chain,
Till only *man* remain."

That is all well, and as it should be in the matter of crown and chain ; but when will the grave cease deepening ? If never, must there not come a time when king and slave drop themselves in, and not even *man* remains? Might it not be a good thing to maintain a while longer social, political, and other distinctions, if only to retard the final catastrophe?

LASTING HAPPINESS EXTRACTED FROM COMMON EXPERIENCES

As the bee distilleth the sweetest honey from wild flowers along the roadside and in meadows, so doth the soul in harmony with God and nature and at peace with itself extract from the common experiences and trivial duties of ordinary life the most wholesome and lasting happiness. Dost thou love beauty? God hath given thee birth in a picture gallery more wonderful than Louvre and Vatican. Hath Heaven attuned thine ear to music? Harken to the clear sweet notes of the bird-song in the tree-tops, the drowsy and delicious chirp of countless insects at nightfall, the murmur of the mountain-brook, the soft sighing of the wind in the leafy retreats of the forest, and the indescribably melodious voices of strong men, beautiful women, and lovely children all around thee. Hath the Creator given thee thirst for knowledge? Nature is an open book, and Pierian springs gush forth on every side. Dost thou hunger for spiritual truth? O child of God, behold the light of truth in the pure life and spotless character of Christ, and gloriously reflected in the humbler lives of His disciples.

NEGLECT

To lips unsanctified by the divine grace of self-renunciation there are few cups more bitter than that of neglect. It bites into even the serene heart of Wisdom to see glittering and tinkling Folly crowned in her place. And yet when the soul has learned to put self aside and to say, "Not my will, but Thine be done!" Gethsemane is peopled with angels, and the bitter cup is changed into a blessed sacrament of peace.

KNOWLEDGE IS NOT ALWAYS POWER

When God holds the cup of life to the lips of youth, He so sweetens the draught that youth and maiden quaff the exhilarating and delicious beverage without suspecting the bitter ingredients held in solution. We should shrink from life, now regarded as so great a boon, could we foresee the perils and hardships of the way. God discloses His goodness in circumscribing our horizons. We sometimes thank Him that we know so much—we ought also to thank Him that we know so little. Knowledge is not always power; on the contrary, it has proved

to many a man the weakest of all his weaknesses. That orderly unfolding of events
without which there could be neither history
nor human enterprise and progress, could not
take place were God to fling wide open the
doors of the future, and bid all men anticipate
His providence.

WITH THE NIGHT COMES REST

It is a sweet and pleasant thought that when
all these days of pain and sorrow and work are
ended—these days of contending and unrest—
there will come the folding of hands. It is
sweet, when sorrow and weariness are our only
companions, to remember that the hour is not far
away when the Father will fold the tired hands
of His child in His, will seal the aching eyes
with sleep, and breathe under their trembling
lids the sweet dream of heaven. Weary not,
nor faint; the Father sees you, and, though
you know it not, His hand leads you. A little
pain and a little labor He metes you for your
good; be patient, and when the night comes
He will give you rest.

MAN'S ONE INALIENABLE RIGHT

Do thy duty and be at peace with God and
thine own conscience. There can be no true

peace for thee apart from the honest and daily
discharge of those obligations, great and small,
which come into thy life from the Creator, and
which, rightly viewed, are angels of divine
discipline. Thou hast too much to say about
thy rights, and thinkest too little about thy
duties. Thou hast but one inalienable right;
and that is the sublime one of doing thy duty
at all times, under all circumstances, and in all
places.

SORROW A PRICELESS TREASURE

Wonderful is the power of great sorrow to
sanctify the heart and purify the life. Under
its influence the most deep-seated prejudices
are dispelled, and the bitter and contentious
heart is completely subdued. No one is fitted
for companionship, much less for the holy
office of friendship, who has not quaffed at
least one wholesome draught from the cup of
affliction. Therefore, O Lord, while my weak
human heart dare not pray for even those
most salutary sorrows which so strengthen
character and clarify spiritual vision, it does
most earnestly entreat that sorrows which
have crossed its path may never be forgotten,
but remain the priceless treasure of a sanctified
memory, and of a pure, believing, and loving
heart.

CULTURE

It is wonderful the large and rich culture that comes to even the most sterile personality when opportunity is improved and power systematically developed. Although the area of Eygpt capable of cultivation is not more than sixteen thousand square miles, only half the area of Ireland, yet Egypt was in the time of the Pharaohs one of the granaries of the world. Ordinary qualities of mind and heart may be cultivated until the desert blossoms as the rose.

SELF-KNOWLEDGE

Self-knowledge must not be confused with mere introspection. There may be much of one where there is little of the other. Introspection separates the man from all that gives him meaning—dissects him as if he were a corpse. Self-knowledge sees him in his many relations—sees him linked in with the universe, and interpreting that universe as it in turn interprets him.

EVERY LIE MUST PERISH

A lie may be delicately clothed in sacerdotal robes; may be descended from apostolic times; may be entrenched behind centuries of Papal and prelatical authority; may be carved in

marble, breathed into music, and overshadowed
by the saints of Raphael and the angels of Fra
Angelico—still a lie is a lie, and in the end
God out of heaven shall smite it dead.

TRUTH MUST BE SOUGHT FOR HER OWN SAKE

Truth must be sought for her own sake.
From all who would find her for private
ends—to establish their own preconceived
opinions or those of their church or party,—
she hides herself in impenetrable darkness.

SEARCH FOR TRUTH AND STRIFE FOR VICTORY

When angry thoughts and impatient words
begin to color your argument, remember that
no two things are more widely sundered than
search for truth and strife for victory.

AUTOINTOXICATION

Never imagine thyself to be what thou art
not, lest the contrast make thee unhappy without rendering thee better. Thou hast no more
right to intoxicate thyself and confuse thine
understanding with idle fancies and silly conceits than with strong drink—both are mockers
and do thee harm. Halo thine head with no
false glory, and burn no sacrilegious incense

before thy soul, but strive to view thyself in
the clear light of truth.

THE UNEDUCATED HEART CANNOT DISCERN
SPIRITUAL BEAUTY

"Never marry but for love ; but see that thou
lovest what is lovely."—*William Penn.*

The advice is good, but somewhat difficult
to follow. If an uneducated eye cannot be
trusted to distinguish genuine beauty from its
cunningly devised counterfeit when both are
presented in marble or upon canvas, how
shall the untrained heart know moral and
intellectual beauty and loveliness when attractive imitations are on every side? One
who is without artistic taste and education
cannot say what is beautiful in art. It is also
true that no one who is devoid of a fine
and noble spiritual development can clearly
discern spiritual beauty in others. The heart,
quite as much as the mind and five senses,
needs to be sent to school; and no education
is worthy of the name that does not include in
its curriculum the enlightenment, guidance, and
discipline of the affections.

WHAT WE UNDERSTAND BY A LIBERAL
EDUCATION

Once by a liberal education was understood

an intimate, sympathetic, and ready acquaintance with all that is best and most attractive
in the opulent storehouse of the world's wisdom.   Later the term came to mean only a
chest of drawers wherein are securely locked
away, all arranged and classified for convenient
reference, the great facts of history, art, science,
and general literature.   "Different matters are
arranged in my head," said Napoleon, "as in
drawers.   I open one drawer and close another,
as I wish."   Now liberal education is rapidly
degenerating into a kind of *index rerum;* it
no longer requires of its possessor any generous
acquaintance with the intellectual treasures of
mankind, but contents itself with exacting of
him a purely mechanical knowledge of how
and where such treasures may be found when
wanted.

NOT ANXIOUS ABOUT A SPIRITUAL CHRIST

Strange it is that men who are so anxious to
find the dead Christ in His tomb, and the
historical Christ in Palestine, care so little for
the spiritual Christ in their own hearts.

"THE TRUTH, THE WHOLE TRUTH, AND NOTHING BUT THE TRUTH"

"The truth, the whole truth, and nothing
but the truth!"   Did ever angel in heaven or

man on earth succeed in telling the truth after that fashion? And yet there is not a little justice of the peace in all the length and breadth of our land who does not feel called upon to demand from every witness who comes before him a divine veracity of which he is himself as incapable as are his fellow-mortals. To hear the lawyers and doctors of divinity discuss, one would think they all had truth and the well in their back yard.

A POOR DESIRE

The desire to say some great thing has prevented the utterance of many a wholesome word, and anxiety to accomplish some wonderful work has crushed in the bud many a humble deed of exceeding grace and sweetness.

THIRTY-FIVE MISCELLANEOUS CHIPS

More strength comes from believing one thing than from doubting a thousand.

Many a whispered word of comfort has awakened a never-ending echo of infinite tenderness.

None are so old as they who have outlived enthusiasm.[1]

[1] A large part of the material contained in this book has been published at various times in English and American papers and magazines. Some of the paragraphs and single

An ounce of enterprise is worth a pound of privilege.

Woe to religion when it ceases to be a matter of faith, and becomes one of mere opinion.

You cannot drink water from an empty cup, neither can you drink the water of life from an empty soul.

The Sacred Writings describe God as a searcher of hearts, but nowhere do they represent Him as a searcher of church records.

Whoever believes there is a difference between a lie and the truth has a creed.

With the loss of Latin as an universal language, all our hope centres in the English Bible and Shakespeare.

"Live while you live" is the motto of thousands who have never lived at all.

There is no medicine in the wisdom of this world that can make a blind eye see God.

sentences have found their way into collections, and have become public property ; and several have been credited by careless writers to other and earlier authors. This sentence appears in Kate Sanborn's *A Year of Sunshine*, as the work of Henry D. Thoreau. The attention of Miss Sanborn was called to the error, and her publishers, Ticknor & Co. of Boston, altered the plate so as to correct the mistake.

To be open to argument and to be open to conviction are two different things.

He has the largest life who lives in the lives of the largest number of people.

Clear discernment and frank acknowledgment of good qualities in a foe are the surest signs of true nobility of character.

Always the lion-heart is a heart of faith.

The Lord demands not "holy orders," but holy men.

The smallest human heart may hold a vast solitude.

A common sorrow makes fast friends.

Pleasure seekers are sorrow finders.

Civilization is the triumph of society.

No defeat is final that does not involve the will.

You can never rejoice in what you do not believe.

Orthodoxy is the heterodoxy of yesterday.

No power on earth or in hell can make a lie immortal.

Character is essentially the power of resisting temptation.

Too large a portion of our modern religion consists in overestimating the apostles and underestimating our neighbors.

He who thinks all good men are of his party must have either a world-wide party or a world-wide conceit of himself.

True peace and deep conviction are inseparable.

The deepest graves are those that hold the living dead.

To-day neglected is to-morrow lost.

It is a man's majestic "Yes!" to the voice of Duty that makes him the man he is.

"Fools rush in where angels fear to tread," and by their very audacity often win for themselves a reward of which the angels never dreamed.

Who would avoid humiliation, let him practise the art of silence.

God only can paint silence, darkness, and a star.

Centres of power are silent.